The Metaphysics of Markets

On

The Metaphysics of Markets

And being an introduction to the philosophy of finance

Simon S Gleadall

St Albans and London, MMX

ISBN 978-1-4461-3737-6

Contents

Preface vii

One   On financial disaster 1

Two   On reacting 31

Three   On the metaphysics of markets 51

Four   On scientific method and trading 89

Five   On moral philosophy 121

Six   On the metaethics of markets 147

Seven   On knowing and markets 177

Eight   Onwards 195

        Notes 205

Preface

This was going to be huge. Brian and the other interns were in the dealing room for the first time and they could feel the tension emanating from the rows of desks, monitors and traders. Everything had being leading up to this moment. The supervisor from HR, after a briefing, told them to spread out and get a feel for the place. The interns tentatively split up.

Brian wandered along a couple of the rows before noticing a trader sitting alone, staring intently at his screen. Seeing the desks either side were empty, Brian felt far less intimidated at the prospect of approaching just this one guy as opposed to a whole team of dealers. Trying to look casual, he ambled towards the trader, who was slouched in his chair and chewing a pencil, his eyes fixed on the flickering screen filled with numbers and charts. As Brian reached the desk, he paused, expecting the trader to look up or notice him. But the trader didn't move. Brian took a deep breath. He wanted to exude confidence. He wanted to be upfront and bullish; the trader would respect him for that, he was sure.

"Hi. I'm a summer intern here and we're just on the dealing floor for this morning and I was wondering if you wouldn't mind telling me what you're trading….what kind of stuff you're doing….if you have a minute…?"

Brian looked directly at the trader, who hadn't stopped concentrating on the screen for an instant. There was a pause of a few seconds and Brian was about to speak, when the trader removed the pencil from his mouth, his eyes still focussed on the screen.

"What's your name?" the trader asked, flatly.

"I'm just an intern here. My name is Brian"

The trader replaced the pencil in his mouth, chewed it some more before taking it out again, eyes always on the monitor.

"Fuck off Brian".

Sometimes learning comes obliquely, but is all the richer for it.

Chapter 1

1.

To trade in the financial markets in the autumn of 2008 was to witness first-hand the greatest destruction of the world's capital stock since 1945. Yet there were no pictures of collapsed buildings nor exploded infrastructure. There were no memorable images to shock the senses, nothing comprehensively tangible to grasp. There was merely a real-time enumeration of the cost of the damage. The typical dealer's newswire terminal displays rising asset prices in green and falling in red. For a very extensive period it felt that any and every portfolio of securities was engulfed in the traditional colour of danger. Stocks, commodities, bonds and almost every currency other than the US dollar fell precipitously; the world's wealth was being shredded. And with the situation at its gravest, it seemed that the catastrophe would be so complete that even those who had profited from the mess could not possibly do so in the final reckoning. Like a pair playing chess on the deck of the Titanic as it struck the iceberg, the question of who is winning or losing at that moment, is rendered futile by the potentially imminent end of their world. It was, for some, extremely exciting.

2.

There is a remarkable degree of agreement concerning the causes of the recent crisis, at least in rough outline, and one wonders whether future historians will share the consensus or if a wholesale revision of the current orthodoxy is inevitable? No doubt there is much to contest in the standard analysis of what occurred, but the most prevalent narrative is one of notable international trade and capital imbalances and massive lending to the Western consumer by the Eastern producer via the purchase of long-dated sovereign debt. The resultant fall in long end interest rates (bond yields) drove investors to chase ever smaller returns at ever greater rates of leverage. And no one group did so more enthusiastically than Western financial institutions who borrowed wholesale at historically minimal rates to lend to homeowners, (those already extant and some newly instantiated) with undue concern for their credit-worthiness on one hand and the susceptibility of the loan collateral (i.e. residential property) to a bursting of the domestic real estate bubble on the other. The process of securitisation whereby mortgages of varying quality could be bundled together, shuffled, and re-traded, allowed the high grade debt to camouflage the low grade (or sub-prime) in a blended portfolio. Credit ratings of these hybrid securities were mistakenly elevated. Typically the mortgages were then traded on to institutions poorly informed, or wilfully ignorant, of their true nature and risk profile. Further fuel was added to the securitisation fire by a massive increase in the issuance and exchange of swap-based over-the-counter (OTC) derivative contracts, again often by institutions (such as insurers) with little historic experience in these products and considerable ignorance of their destructive potential. Combinations of debt, derivatives and credit default swaps convinced some shareholders, managers and regulators that the risks were not merely contained but were mutually mitigating. Events swiftly proved the contrary to be true; the amalgamation of instruments was incendiary rather than dampening. The dubious off-balance sheet accounting entities known as Special Investment Vehicles (SIVs) had only served to divert attention away from the real debt-equity ratios of lenders. The system started to work against itself.

Rising real estate prices had provided the perpetuating momentum to the system and the inflexion point of summer 2007 marked the beginning of the crisis. The capital markets went from an inundation of cash to a drought with a rapidity few had anticipated or priced in. The opaqueness of many balance sheets suddenly cleared;

lenders entirely dependent on cheap, virtually limitless wholesale funding found the wells were dry, their loans were turning bad and the recoverable collateral was devaluing. This simple combination was poisonous enough, but compounded in toxicity by the revealed interconnectedness of the *dramatis personae*. Within a year the entire financial and monetary system faced collapse as it became clear that confidence was so drained that no institution would survive, regardless of their exposure to the initial underlying problems.

The annihilation of the monetary system was apparently avoided by massive, coordinated Governmental action to act as guarantor, to re-capitalise and to make available limitless short term liquidity to the institutions that remained. Within months the destruction of confidence and squeeze on credit sent economies into dramatic declines. Unemployment rose steadily and monetary and fiscal measures were employed globally to avert depression.

This narrative might find critics. Certainly it is a simplification. And yet I shall make very little effort to defend this account since the key argument I wish to sustain rests upon a claim as to the true course of recent history that need not be overly strong. No doubt quite rightly, for many decades to come, economists, historians and finance theorists will look to uncover the true story of what occurred and why. For my part however, I need rely upon a claim that is altogether weaker and therefore, as is true of all weak claims, can only be refuted by a far stronger counter-claim.[1] The point that I hope will find acceptance and avoid excessive controversy from the outset is that with regards to our financial markets we are in something of a pickle. Even the most optimistic of theorists and practitioners would surely concede that what has occurred has been deeply unpleasant, undesirable and unwelcome. It would be an extreme position to hold that the recent crisis has been a jolly good thing, *of itself*. Beware the distinction between the event and consequence here. To argue for the desirability of the consequence is not necessarily to welcome the events *per se*. So, one might own that an unwinding of leverage is to be welcomed, without demanding the near-collapse of the financial system in the process. All that I profess as an acceptable summation of recent events, and as a premise hereafter, is that we are in something of a bind with regards to our financial markets and institutions and their relation to the rest of society.

3.

The generation of financiers found wanting by an adherence to awry economic thought, erroneous financial theory and a collective myopia have been decidedly upstaged by the insight and counsel proffered by historians. The traders whose decisions were guided by extrapolation from mere months of data were struck dumb and lectured to by historians who dealt in little less than decades. Politicians turned to central bankers, regulators and to the bankers themselves seeking relevant wisdom. Of course they could see to some extent what had been brewing, but the asset bubbles had been too politically expedient to attempt a pre-emptive pricking. Swiftly, the necessity of action as opposed to inaction was unanimously agreed upon. As the banks most exposed to a collapse in property values and a dearth in liquidity in short term paper wobbled, two inherent weaknesses of the system became evident. Firstly, that the web of institutions was so tightly weaved that their exposures were not merely similar or directionally aligned, but sharing of a fundamental characteristic, namely a fatal co-dependence. A risk considered forgettable beforehand was that the embedded assumption belying every institution's position (that the system itself was sustainable) would hold *no matter what*. Secondly, many years of consolidation had left a few dominant players in the investment banking arena. This power grab had enlarged balance sheets and enabled ever-greater leveraging to occur, whilst displaying a diversified veneer. But as this cracked, it became clear that many institutions had become a *necessary* part of the system and that their individual collapse would be a sufficient detonation to explode the network in its entirety.

And so the course of action ran approximately thus. As preliminary distress emerged in mid-2007, large scale liquidity was added to the short-term lending market by central banks. Overnight interest rates were reduced. By mid-2008 the crisis was gathering pace as Bear Stearns had faced insolvency and been subsumed by JP Morgan. Endless short term liquidity was made available. By some, this was viewed as methadone being given freely to heroin addicts in preference to cold turkey. But historians suggested the application of the latter in 1929 in like circumstance, conferred status on the former as the lesser of two evils.

Monetarists and Keynesians resumed their unending dispute, advising monetary expansion and a slashing of borrowing rates on one hand and a massive fiscal stimulus (via tax cuts and/or the hastening of public sector fixed capital formation) on the other. In the event, much of this debate became moot in the short term as authorities threw everything at the problem. In the UK alone, benchmark interest rates fell 525 basis points in 18 months and the digital printing press conjured up in excess of 200 billion pounds to purchase gilt-edged (sovereign bond) securities from institutions by the Bank of England. Meanwhile, Governments cut direct and indirect taxes, subsidised motor vehicle purchases and certain residential real estate buying. They offered both tacit and explicit insurance to various industrial borrowing and even to personal mortgages for those in arrears and newly unemployed.

In all, trillions of dollars of funds were injected either temporarily (in theory) via the printing press or permanently by colossal additions to national deficits. Interest rate reductions were coordinated by disparate central banks for greater psychological impact. No-one can claim that the severity of the situation was not ultimately recognised.

Broadly then this describes the actions taken. The principle lessons of previous crises were noted, namely that liquidity and fiscal stimulus were necessary to avoid immediate catastrophe. The domestic pressures for protectionism were foreseen and duly acknowledged whilst overwhelmingly resisted beyond mere pacifying tokenism. The need to defend banks explicitly was deemed paramount. Initial attempts at the latter foundered as the plan to simply purchase toxic assets was muddied and supported flailing branches rather than wobbling trunks. Banks thus supported, many of whose shares had hitherto lost 90% of their value, soared in price. But the effects of the systematic earthquake were feeding through by late 2008 to the non-financial economy. World-wide output slumped and deep recession took hold. By the summer of 2009 most economies had technically exited recession, although the extent to which this was mere asset reflation was unclear.

Turning to the more general question then of how 'we' have reacted. Of course most people have just attempted to continue living their lives. Many or most 'got angry' with 'bankers'; few seemed to believe culpability lay anywhere else. But despite professed revulsion, there were no riots or episodes of civil unrest beyond those typically accompanying international economic G-summits. Yet the events have affected everyone to a greater or lesser extent, whether economically or psychologically. The elected and non-elected representatives of the world's peoples certainly seemed to show a global solidarity or at least a professed commitment to work together. Prominence was given to the select handful of economists, bankers and hedge fund managers who had forewarned of the crisis (in some cases perpetually and for so long that one wonders how great a credit is due to their prognostications). Motivated by the pressing nature of the potential effects of the banking system's collapse, efforts took an overwhelmingly reactive approach, targeted firmly at the consequential face of the crisis. Attempts to identify and address the causes were, correctly, relegated in importance in the first instance by governments. A vitriolic press demanded vengeful action against bankers, notably not via judicial process (as it was far from obvious that many actual crimes had been committed), but rather via attempts to demonise and affect their re-numeration. Very little of the animosity manifested itself in direct undertakings by the disaffected, although an armed guard was temporarily mounted in Connecticut at the offices of AIG and Sir Fred Goodwin, erstwhile CEO of the Royal Bank of Scotland, left the country following vandalism at his Edinburgh home.

After the initial bailouts, arbitrary restrictions were mooted for banks recipient of state funding, such as a $500,000 ceiling on banker compensation. Sensing the potential long term recriminatory effects of accepting Treasury assistance (and in particular with regards to the loss in self-determination and the right to set compensation levels independently), institutions avoided funds that were not forced upon them. Others sought finance elsewhere, from private sources and also from Middle or Far Eastern sovereign wealth funds.[2] The broad consensus was that many, if not all financial institutions would have failed without the emergency reserves and stake-holding of domestic governments. A modicum of stability returned to the monetary system, albeit without an accompanying and convincing relaxing of the flow of intra-institutional funds.

The points to note here are not the specifics of the actions taken; the whys and wherefores of this fiscal package or that monetary easing. This background story has been provided as a means to an end, which is to suggest that there is a particular, striking characteristic pervading all of this activity. An essential aspect of the response to the crisis is its having been formulated and exacted in what may be termed a philosophical vacuum. That is to say, the effort made to mitigate the emerging disaster was devoid of any framework of thought beyond a simplistic economic and political knee-jerk. And this continues to be the case some years into the drama. The consequences of this shallow-mindedness are likely to be extremely grave unless addressed directly. To understand the reasons why this has been our seemingly instinctive reaction requires a deep historical understanding and a profound sense of the cultural roots of modern capitalist finance. But before considering this, an explanation is due as to what is meant by the claim that the backdrop to the crisis has no adequate philosophical foundation.

4.

King John I of England was not, by many standards of decency, a good man: a murderer, a serial bungler in military matters, someone who betrayed his family repeatedly and who was ultimately excommunicated by the Pope. But some historians are happy to offset these negatives at least in part by his supposedly excellent proficiency in the administration of his realm; secretarial prowess indeed that in any way serves to redeem a life of seemingly endless wrongdoing, ill-judgement and calamity. Born in 1167 to King Henry II and Eleanor of Aquitaine, John stood to inherit, by virtue of his being their youngest son, precisely nothing, receiving in consequence his first epithet, John Lackland. As Henry had supposedly foreseen in his commission of a painting showing young eagles devouring their father, two of his sons (Richard and the hapless John) did indeed later rise up against him. On his death in 1189, Richard (who, it stark juxtaposition, would become known as the Lionheart) acceded to the throne and embarked on the Third Crusade in partnership with Phillip II of France. In an age of rife instability and mutual mistrust, the two would take the Cross and crusade together or not at all, lest the monarch left in arrears usurped the other's kingdom or territorial domain. On returning from a tricky campaign against the armies of Saladin, Richard was kidnapped in 1192 by Leopold V of Austria and held to ransom for a colossal sum (possibly several times the annual revenue Richard's kingdom afforded him). His brother John, who in his crusading absence had ruled England (with little enthusiasm from the King's subjects) promptly entered into negotiations with the hostage-takers. In a startling display of diplomacy and characteristically abominable duplicity he attempted to broker a deal whereby payment would be made to the kidnappers on condition that Richard's captivity would continue.

By 1194, Richard and John's mother Eleanor had raised the demanded ransom and Richard returned to England for what was presumably a frosty re-union with his brother. But the Lionheart proved worthy of the name and offered John full forgiveness and even consented to his being appointed heir to the throne. On Richard's death in 1199, John became King despite some protestation, and his reign lurched from one disaster to the next. His alleged involvement in the disappearance of his nephew Arthur (rumoured to have been personally castrated by John and dumped in the River Seine) led to massive uprisings against his rule in France. In fairness, Arthur, at the time of his capture by John, was trying to kidnap his own grandmother, John's mother Eleanor. And yet, a succession of defeats cost John vast tracts of his Kingdom and necessitated unprecedented amounts of taxation. A second unflattering epithet followed as he failed to quell uprisings; John Softsword. And as unlikely as the prospect seemed, matters were about to worsen considerably for John's sorely tried subjects. The King disputed the appointment by Pope Innocent III of the new Archbishop of Canterbury. The situation escalated until the Pope issued a full Papal Interdiction on England.

It is difficult, some 800 years hereafter, to appreciate how truly awful this outcome must have been for the general populace. In an age of short life expectancy, high infant mortality and punishing poverty, religious salvation and specifically a far superior afterlife, were to many the only solace this earthly life afforded. The interdiction meant six years of closed churches and very few baptisms, consecrated burials or sanctified marriages; devastating to a faithful flock.

Even at this late stage, John could have turned things around. His reputation might have had more something far more persuasive than just bureaucratic competence as its saving grace. How differently would Bad King John be remembered had he marched forthrightly to Runnymede near Windsor and demanded the drawing up of the Great Charter (or Magna Carta)? But true to character, the King went unwillingly and under duress; at the insistence of his thoroughly disgruntled barons. Yet in that soggy meadow (the runny mede) he approved, by royal seal, what became one of the true milestones in the story of human liberty, political emancipation and philosophical statements on freedom.

John did not quite grasp this 'bigger picture'. For him, the Magna Carta represented an outrage against his Godly Kingship, an unlawful restriction on his power and (perhaps most insidiously) a serious diminution of his tax raising powers. Within a year John reneged on the deal. He entered into a full civil war against his baronetcy, during which he died. But not before he had lost all the crown jewels trying to cross the Wash, in perhaps a fitting symbolism.

5.

There is very little about the detention centre at Guantanamo Bay which is un-contentious and, obvious acts of terrorism and war aside, of a scenario that has created greater global controversy in the past decade. It is a matter debated in highly polarised terms. It becomes clear why this should be so once one considers the difficulty in establishing an agreeable conceptual framework within which discussion is possible. There are great claims made for the rights of certain persons or of collectives; the right of the detainees to due legal process or the right of the United States to defend itself as it sees fit. There are claims made for and against the international *legality* of the detention process, a dispute which can be reduced to factual disagreement as to events but moreover to disparate understanding regarding the *nature* of the persons involved. So the detainees are labelled variously as unlawful combatants, jihadists, soldiers, terrorists or innocent men hitherto not proven guilty. Consensus must necessarily elude when basic terms are not merely different but contradictory. The probable consequences of the centre's existence have been endlessly discussed and long term detriment is often pitched against short term expediency. Theoretical moral considerations (in particular those of liberalism) are posited as trumping mere practical convenience. But pragmatists reject the relegation of their concerns if the un-tried detainees are who the US government say they are ("Bad people" according to Dick Cheney); releasing people from captivity who are intent on your annihilation is plain stupid, they might claim.

This matter is complicated for many reasons. There is an intricate blend of legal, moral, historical and practical difficulties which need to be addressed and may be mutually conflicting. Here is a situation of grave importance to a country and its citizens from a pragmatic standpoint and one of obvious relevance to those held in captivity without trial. How then do we approach such scenarios which have international ramifications and deeply symbolic ethical connotations? The answer is that we are guided by more than the immediate physical or actual outcomes or prospects from our decisions. We do not, generally, merely look to the real-world consequence likely to be manifested by our choices. A more enlightened procedure aims to take better account of the wider philosophical context of the matter at hand. This case is complex because the identities of those involved are not clear-cut. By identities is not meant simply the names of the people and countries involved but their very essence; the nature of who they are. It is this lack of clarity that in turn makes their legal status and the corresponding obligations beholden of their captors opaque. The debate quickly becomes metaphysical; that is to say it looks at the nature of the existence of those concerned. Any discussion of rights and duties is contingent upon identities being robustly demarcated.

The Magna Carta approved by King John in 1215 marks an important milestone in the history of the legal concept of *habeas corpus* since it is a very clear and early written promulgation as to the rights of a captee. It is professed without any associated proof of its objective truth; it is simply stated as an accepted article of law, that any prisoner has the right to a judicial explanation literally *justifying* his incarceration. The issues surrounding the Guantanamo Bay detention centre transcend the undoubtedly important practical outcomes. An argument is made that the men were captured fighting American troops unlawfully, under the colours of no particular nation, and that they are bent of the destruction of the US army, nation and way of life and should therefore not be released. To some this makes a simple and compelling case for the men's indefinite imprisonment without trial. The reason that this argument lacks complete cogency, however, is that it is at best overly simplistic or worse, truly fallacious, from a philosophical standpoint. Consider the many assumptions that belie this argument that must simply be accepted at face value for us to be persuaded. The facts surrounding the circumstances of someone's capture are always relevant, since capture must logically precede detention. The very charge against these men is entwined in the occasion of their capture. Are they nation-less soldiers arrested on the battlefield itself or unfortunate civilian bystanders caught up in the war? This is just one way in which the guilt is an assumption of this argument as well as the conclusion. The most elementary counter-factual defence ("I was not fighting") is overlooked by this argument. But other doubts remain. In what sense were these men fighting illegally? These are not mere matters of definition or meeting certain international standards. Was the US attack on Afghanistan against the ruling executive and its armed forces? So they might claim, but what if those whose territory is attacked see it is a far wider assault? Did the US see 9/11 as an attack specifically on Wall Street by Al Qaeda? Of course it did not. The difficulty here is that the captors of the detainees are imposing their own characterisation as to whom and what they were fighting and they are using this as the existential qualification in deciding the applicability of the notion of *habeas corpus*.

The sanctity of the right to petition a writ of *habeas corpus* is not universally accepted of course. As mentioned, no formal proof has been successfully offered such as to carve the right in stone. Historically the right is often removed or suspended in times of national emergency, as in the case of the Guantanamo Bay detention centre or during the Troubles in Northern Ireland in the latter half of the 20th century. In August, 1971 *habeas corpus* rights were denied to Irish prisoners *suspected* of IRA involvement and a number of high profile, extensive detentions without trial occurred. Oftentimes the ethical doubtfulness of this action is accompanied by concerns as to the practical, longer term effects, insofar as the benefit to the captors of possible safety from harm by the captee's incarceration comes at a cost of the figurative or literal martyrdom of the detainee to the cause. There can also be a cost in the perceived or veritable weakening of the moral authority of the detainer.

In short, when assessing the validity of the action of a State to detain people indefinitely without judicial process, we acknowledge that a situation has arisen of a socially complex and deeply human nature. We realise that there are real and pragmatic consequences to the decisions made, but that these should rarely act as the sole guide to our discretion. Instead, we normally adopt an attitude that tries to account for historical precedent and ethical evaluations. We try to encompass an assessment of the true, underlying nature of the parties and concepts involved. We clarify terms. We debate every element of the situation and attempt to justify our actions from the basic premises which we hold to be true.

It was with such a mindset that President Obama declared that "The individuals currently detained at Guantanamo have the constitutional privilege of the writ of *habeas corpus*" and ordered the detention centre's closure. A clear intellectual path may be drawn through history from this statement to Bad King John in a soggy field some 800 years before.

6.

"I love life, Mr President", wrote Piergiorgio Welby, as he asked to be allowed to die. The muscular dystrophy that had been diagnosed when he was 17 had claimed his last movable finger in April, 2006, leaving him with a single eyelid with which to control his computer, his only real outlet to the world. On 21 September, the Italian poet wrote his open letter to Giorgio Napolitano, President of the Republic, wanting "to obtain euthanasia", which was illegal in Italy.

Suicide is a matter that strikes at the very core of our humanity and existence. Camus saw it as the primary issue to resolve before meaningful questions about life can even begin to be asked.[3] Is suicide right, wrong or indeed necessary? And yet for all its importance, few matters can have encountered so little consensus across times, places and cultures. Suicide has been viewed variously as a crime and mortal sin but, as often, as an act of the highest virtue and magnanimity.

The traditional ethical difficulties of suicide have been compounded by advances in medicine. Modern science can sustain the ravaged body for great lengths of time in some cases, possibly long after the unfortunate patient has lost consciousness, cognitive power or the will to live. The consequences of suicide could hardly be more profound. So how then does society approach a matter of this importance?

Suicide of any kind remains illegal in much of the world. In times past, the obvious impossibility of punishing the offender found the family of the deceased liable, no doubt often heaping misery on misery. Forfeiture of the dead person's estate to the Crown was commonplace in England. Sir William Blackstone (1723-1780), a professor and chronicler of English law , would presumably have seen this as fully just reparation as his Commentaries on the Laws of England denounce suicide as "a double offence" against God and the King, "who hath interest in the preservation of all his subjects". Blackstone offers no justification for this moral judgement and an obvious defence might be mounted by a Republican atheist against such condemnation (or more precisely by a deceased Republican atheist's lawyer).

Blackstone's influence, particularly on early American law, can hardly be over-stated. The four volumes of his Commentaries provided the expanding colonies with practical and portable works of reference, in some cases the only such written guide to law physically available. This, and of course a strongly Christian absolute condemnation of suicide, has guided much of the Western world to its current stance.

Science has much to contribute to the debate; and increasingly so. From psychology, we have the assertion that suicide is a permanent solution to a temporary problem. As depressive mental states are better understood and the compounding impact of substance abuse is recognised, it becomes hard not to see many suicides as tragic and certainly sub-optimal outcomes, rather than as romanticized acts of great philosophical import or as ultimate expressions of self-determination. We might suppose that distinctions can be made as to the various causes of suicide although this is trickier than one might think. On the face of it, someone who, with all clarity of thought, wishes to commit suicide due to a progressively worsening medical condition seems very different from someone extremely unhappy due to circumstance or internal chemical imbalances. But the dividing line is not so simply drawn; the difficulty is in determining an absolute notion of clear-headedness. If the temporarily depressive feels suicidal we might suggest they are not thinking straight at this moment in time. But the very same line of thought applies to the apparently rational, physically degenerative person. The improvements in medicinal care – in pharmacology and human biology – offer hope to some of the most seriously ill or injured, yet this can be a double-edged sword, since the body can sometimes be preserved beyond such time as the mind ceases to will it. As the cognitive sciences advance from their current infancy, they bear the promise of ever-greater understanding of the suicidal tendency. If one believes many suicides to run counter to a person's long term interest (and intuitively this seems reasonable), then one ought to welcome any such insight as might lead to aversion.

Cultural attitudes to suicide exhibit remarkable divergence across time and place. Ritual suicidal practises were commonplace in Classical Mediterranean societies and in medieval feudal Japan. But whereas the Western secular societies have since largely revoked any lingering sentiment associating suicide with nobility (presumably due to the erstwhile influence of Christianity), its resonance in contemporary Japanese culture is far stronger. Doubtless this owes much to the extreme ritualistic self-killing that formed part of the *bushido*, the samurai code of honour that influenced their personal conduct from the 8th century A.D. to the 19th. For hundreds of years and as recently as the late 19th century, dishonoured warriors could save face by performing ritual *seppuku*. The samurai would write his death poem before thrusting his short sword into his own abdomen and immediately thereafter being all but decapitated by their Second (often a friend). Such action was expected in the line of duty for offences ranging from defeat on the battlefield to petty criminality. It is not hard to see how such extraordinary behaviour over a sustained period of time would leave something of an impression on the national psyche. And Japan of course firmly re-acquainted itself with suicidal practices in its deployment of kamikaze fighter pilots in World War II. These truly desperate acts were supposedly borne initially of a deficit in aviation fuel. But the heroic status afforded in some quarters to the pilots and its obvious connection to the old warrior class further mythologized the notion of honourable self-destruction.

One might consider a strictly *analytic* approach to an inquiry into the nature of suicide and its moral connotations. That is, to give consideration to the very terminology of the matter. If homicide is the killing of a human, and murder the same but with ill-intentioned forethought, is suicide (self-killing) identical to self-murder? This is more than mere semantic gaming, for it is very much this reading of suicide that allows Blackstone to declare that suicide should be "ranked among the highest crimes, making it a peculiar species of felony, a felony committed on one's self". A corollary is that even someone who advises suicide "is guilty of murder". But on closer inspection there seems to be a problem with the logic of equating suicide to self-murder. Surely murder must preclude the acquiescence of the victim or else it seems indistinct from assisted suicide? But this then gives the argument a displeasing circularity, for clearly the victim of a suicide acquiesces to the murderer's (i.e. his own) intention. This seems then to reduce suicide to assisted suicide of oneself, which is either absurd or vacuous. This is most damaging to claims that suicide is a serious crime. Its direct association with murder makes a compelling case for the act's immorality, so the strength of the link is essential to those who condemn it on this count.

This brief and simplified analysis hints at the contribution philosophical thinking can make to such debates. By considering the precise meaning of the language and concepts that frame the situation at hand, it can draw out the paradoxes of our everyday conclusions. It encourages us to tread with greater trepidation and edifies the logical weaknesses of our positions. Note, it may offer no definite alternative to our stance which it may have proven inconsistent. This is certainly the negative face of philosophy. Yet for all that, it allows us to proceed knowing we do so imperfectly and mindful of the need to strive for ever greater robustness. This in itself is a valuable contribution.

With very few notable exceptions, the majority of the world's religions condemn suicide. Although the Bible makes no specific statement against the practice *per se*, it is often presumed to fall within the scope of the commandment not to murder (or kill depending on the religious denomination in question). It is however explicitly forbidden by the Churches of all denominations. 4:29 in the Koran is usually taken as clear condemnation of self-killing, bringing to mind the brazen acts of jihadist suicide bombers to the contrary. Pope Benedict XVI referred to "the inviolable dignity of human life, from conception to its natural end" in asserting the Roman Catholic doctrinal position regarding such matters. The irony was not lost on Piergiorgio Welby, as he wrote via a computer that scanned his flickering eyelid and breathed, as he had for 12 years, involuntarily by artificial respirator. "What is natural about a hole in the belly and a pump that fills it with fats and proteins? What is natural about a hole in the windpipe and a pump that blows air into the lungs?" The Church of course was not for turning and would later deny Welby a Christian funeral.

The subset of suicides that are assisted also raises difficult questions about the nature of doctoring. Welby's own case is illustrative; it was ruled that he had the constitutional right to refuse treatment (i.e. his respirator could be switched off by his doctor on request) but the doctor would then be legally obliged to attempt to resuscitate him. This apparent contradiction or absurdity is but one of many such difficulties in this area. For example, it is often stated that the medic's first rule is 'to do no harm' (this is often mistakenly traced back to the Hippocratic Oath). This seems trivial in standard cases, but diminishingly so as the illness becomes more chronic. What constitutes harm in the most serious of cases? Prolonging a life of suffering seems to run counter to the rule, but then ending a life seems the most fundamental breach of the rule. The difficulty here is conceptual, in the sense of what a doctor really is and ought to do and what is truly meant by 'harm'. Religious considerations aside, there seems a strong case for permitting assisted suicide when certain conditions are met, which might include the patient's lucid wishes being independently verifiable, the magnitude of suffering clearly being great and the prospect of recovery miniscule or nil. Yet there remains much opposition, even in many broadly secular societies to its legitimisation. The predominant reason for this is usually some form of consequentialist fear. If euthanasia is permitted, the case of Piergiorgio Welby may prove the thin end of a wedge whereby pressure may be brought to bear on the elderly or sick to 'do the decent thing'. It is also suggested that it would radically alter the nature of doctoring. This latter point is often made in the face of a tacit acceptance that euthanasia is indeed regularly practised; a doctor may give large doses of painkillers ostensibly to relieve pain, but in the knowledge that death could or will be a side-effect. The morality of such action then largely becomes a question of motivation.

Let us look to the general character of the problems of suicide and societal reactions thereon. Firstly, it should be clear that this is indeed a sphere of human existence and life which is problematic for society. Suicide is a widespread practice, with intense repercussions for the principal character, his family and friends. Suicides can cluster and publicity of one is thought to encourage others. In short, this is a serious issue for society to address. How then do we proceed? The answer seems to be illogically, inconsistently and inadequately. But this probably just reflects the complexity of the matter. In trying to achieve a modicum of understanding or insight as a society with regards to suicide, our approach is practical, scientific, political, cultural, theological, philosophical and ethical. If one considers the nature of the debate that still occurs very readily (as in the cases of Piergiorgio Welby in Italy or Terri Schiavo in the US), we find all the tools of these fields and crafts of human reasoning put to work. Scientists work to improve medical care such that suffering may be diminished or ended; psychologists study the emotional causes of depression and anxieties which seem so often in attendance in non-euthanasia suicide cases. We are strongly influenced by our cultural perspective on the matter, which may range from revulsion to admiration. Our religious beliefs, or legacy thereof, may dictate or guide our moral attitude to the matter. The certitude of Papal decree makes the issue one of great simplicity for the Faithful; suicide is wrong because the Pope says it is displeasing to God. Politicians must account for such sensitivities and balance all these inputs whilst remaining mindful of the great practical complexities that individual cases may entail. The role of doctors in the case of assisted suicides is considered from a philosophical standpoint and the Hippocratic Oath may be invoked as a source of historical authority in a similar vain to the invocation of Magna Carta with respect to emancipation.

In time a consensus may, or may not, be reached. The practice may be made illegal or tolerated, discouraged or honoured. Religious authority may win out or totalitarian executives may simply draw lines in the sand as they see fit. Technological progress and scientific advances may alter the very facts of the matter. Any 'solution' to the 'problem' of suicide is likely to always incite controversy and altercation. But despite such untidiness it is overwhelmingly the case that we attend to a matter of this gravity as thoughtfully and soberly as is humanly possible. To a great extent, it is the very nature of humanity to do so.

On 20 December, 2006 Dr Mario Riccio confirmed to his own satisfaction that Piergiorgio Welby was fully cognisant and wanted to die. Risking up to 15 years in prison, he sedated the poet and removed his attachments. 40 minutes later, Welby passed away. Riccio was cleared of wrongdoing in February 2007.

7.

The preceding accounts of approaches that can be taken to deal with the array of complexities arising from questions of individual liberty and the killing of one's self are particular instances of a general methodology applied in a variety of situations. This method has philosophy at its heart, and by philosophy is meant a system of thoughtful enquiry. Our reasoning and emotive capacities distinguish us from other animals more essentially than any other points of difference. Whether either our rational or emotional faculty (or some combination thereof) motivates our actions, we can scarcely doubt that we act without due cause. Why did I tune in to Radio 3 and not Radio 4 today? Perhaps I desired to hear music rather than speech and reasoned that Radio 3 (which in the main is a music station) would be a better bet than Radio 4 (which in the main is not). This is the account David Hume would likely support; our motivation *is* our desire and our reason thereafter deals with the practicalities of fulfilling this desire. Now whether this theory is accurate is beside the current point. What matters is that a narrative may be constructed to explain what occurred. A most intuitively implausible account is one stating that everything we do has absolutely no logical causal motivation.

Doubtless our motivations are complex at an individual and societal level. But only an ardent nihilist or perhaps randomist would argue that there are no motivating forces belying our actions. So if we accept that we act for reasons (and by this is meant due to certain causes rather than by virtue of our reasoning faculties), then it is suggested that at heart these reasons can always be considered philosophically. That is to say, we can make enquiry as to what causal processes are at work, the nature of the concepts in use and the status and essence of the agents involved.

Consider the notion of *habeas corpus* as framed by the Magna Carta. This exhibits a sophistication of philosophical thought with regards to the nature of monarchy, the ontology of individual rights and the existence of limits to State power. It is quite impossible to justify an individual's right to petition for a writ of *habeas corpus* without having a clear analysis in mind of the relevant conceptual structure. No case can be made for *habeas corpus* as a right without first having an understanding or presumption of the nature of such rights. No debate on the limit of monarchic power is possible without an accompanying discussion regarding the fundamental meaning of monarchy. Our attitudes to such matters are likely to evolve; the existence of objective truth ever debatable. Yet in issues of great import involving liberty and death, a higher order of thinking is a fundamental pre-requisite to any serious debate. Even if our judgements seem coldly prosaic and concerned in the final reckoning with everyday practicalities, the philosophical context will rarely be entirely lost. This is quite clearly seen if one extends the sample from the two previous specific situations to broader scenarios.

Consider the multifarious systems of governance in current operation and those seemingly obsolete from earlier civilisations. Societies may arrive at their current set-up by violence, imposition or oppression but also by an (often subsequent) emancipation, consensus, revolution or a change of heart in the ruling body. Today it is possible to find democracy, dictatorship, neo-Marxism, theocracy and absolutist monarchy co-existing in various states of happiness. In each case however, a philosophical system of thought is in evidence which makes explicit or implicit claims as to the nature of say human rights or the existence and will of a divine being. It will, for example, presume in claiming legitimacy to have settled matters (in some sense) pertaining to ownership, the right to claim property as private and the rights and obligations of persons within the framework of the state.

The history of such matters in England is not untypical: from Neolithic tribalism and regional kingdoms to subjugation and occupation under Roman rule; from kingship and medieval feudalism to the emergence of nationhood, Civil War, Glorious Revolution and adoption of constitutional monarchy in the 17th century; the rise of urban majorities and a middling class; the relative decline of landowning class influence coincidental with industrialisation; the demands for extensive suffrage and truer representation. This vast, meandering history one might dare to label progressive. And every evolutionary twist, every claim to know better and every appeal for a more just political outcome, is accompanied by deep philosophical argument being brought to bear. Enlightened or reasoned assertions tend to be built upon previously worked claims. Mill's powerful statement on liberty for example (the 'harm principle') "that the only purpose for which power can be rightfully exercised over any member of a civilized community, against his will, is to prevent harm to other. His own good, either physical or moral, is not a sufficient warrant", did not emerge from the ether, brilliant though he was. It owes a debt to antecedent intellectual endeavour by Locke, Hobbes, Bacon and hundreds or thousands more besides. Nothing comes from nothing in this sense.

An enquiring approach that questions at every level what exists, what concepts may be taken to mean and what is inherently presumed, has been, in the most part, an extremely productive methodology and it is not of course limited in scope to any one aspect of life or human experience. Any subject that can be conceived has a philosophical branch which asks fundamental questions about the subject itself. So if art is the subject concerned perhaps with artistry, the output of artists, the forms of creativity and the history of art, the *philosophy* of art deals with questions of what is meant by art, what we can know about art, whether there is a correct method of art etc. etc. When controversy arises it is often recourse to these fundamentals that allows the parameters of the debate to be constructed. How often one hears post-modern art decried as 'not real art'. Almost immediately in this case the questions raised are metaphysical and require philosophical elucidation. Attempts to answer them will require employment of tried and trusted philosophical apparatus; the tools of logic, deduction, induction, distinction, contradiction and sound reasoning.

Everyday difficulties that people encounter rarely require such deep probing. It is often sufficient to accept concepts as given, definitions as workable and proceed from there. Even in cases where the morality of an action is unclear, the usual approach is not to ponder *ad nauseam*, but to rely upon the wisdom of experience, common-sense and intuition to assess the likely outcomes of action or inaction and to make a decision. But in the case of large scale enterprise, of a grand undertaking that may span generations, it is well worth investing time to try to verify the foundations. And no subject has turned the lens of philosophy on itself more keenly that that which has perhaps greater claim than most to being labelled its pre-eminent successor: science.

The philosophy of science is a highly developed branch of both disciplines and this perhaps should not be surprising as natural philosophy constituted modern science's direct ancestry. Experimental science familiar to us today has its roots not so much in Aristotle (whose observational cataloguing was neither controlled nor repetitive in the modern scientific sense) but in Empiricism; the 17th and 18th centuries' philosophical acceptance of sense experience as an acceptable path to knowledge. The limits and admissibility of induction; metaphysical questions regarding the meaning of causality; the search for a distinction between science and other systems' claims to knowledge (such as astrology for example); much thought has been given to such matters with great progress made. Once again, the sum total benefit of such work is not merely in answering the set questions; it is as much in drawing out the limits and problems of scientific work itself. It encourages caution and continually demands rigorous attention to First Principles.

Art and science are not alone in receiving this attention. Almost any subject one cares to name has been considered philosophically. From Frege in the 1870s, mathematicians began to fear that their theory was running ahead of itself and before the foundational concrete had set. Through Russell, Whitehead, Moore and others, mathematics was re-cast as formal philosophical logic. By stepping back from the subject in this way, it was hoped that a small set of self-evident axioms could be posited, from which, by logical deduction, *any* theory of mathematics could be irrefutably reached. This would furnish the subject with maximum robustness and provide a sure-footing for mathematicians to follow for all time; a most noble sentiment of academic methodology. But it was not to be, as one of the 20th century's greatest intellectual achievements was to demonstrate. In 1931, the 25 year old Kurt Gödel published his Incompleteness Theorem which dashed Russell et al's hopes. Very loosely, since the detail is extraordinarily esoteric, the theorem demonstrated by formal logic that no system of axioms can ever be proved to be fully consistent, *by use of the axioms themselves*. One cannot provide a set of axioms that are self-evidently true that can be used to prove the truth of the statement *"This system of axioms is fully consistent"*. This was unfortunate in one light but still achieved the general goal of solidifying the basis of mathematics; the result may not have been in the manner of the one originally hoped for, but the philosophical consideration given to the problem meant that the limits of mathematical foundations would forever be apparent.

Jurisprudence is the philosophy of law. The practical importance of the Rule of Law needs little re-iteration. But laws are temporary and often inadequate approximations as to what society considers acceptable conduct. Furthermore, the obeyance of certain behaviour to a given law can only be judged by an imprecise theory of correspondence. For example, if a law prevents say libelous journalism, the prosecutor must satisfy the judge or jury that the accused's behaviour matched that prohibited by the law. In other words, for any malfeasance to be prosecutable, the correspondence between a specific action and a generic conceptualized undesirable action must be assumed possible. Reaching *any* sort of verdict has the possibility of this correspondence as a premise. Surely in few areas of life is the precision of the language more paramount, as it is by resort to legal process that many vital disputes are bought to resolution. Whether it is Anglo-American common law, Franco-Germanic (derivative of Roman) statute law, Islamic sharia or despot-dictated law that is in use, all are philosophically under-pinned and have been analyzed in a way that has a great bearing on individual cases or on the colour and code of the laws themselves. And when laws are amended or added to the statute book, it may be as a result of circumstantial changes to contemporary life (e.g. the influence of new knowledge, a change in an ethical disposition) or due to a more fundamental conceptual re-interpretation. Jurisprudence will feature heavily in both cases.

So any particular field that inquisitive humans wish to contemplate may be studied both directly and abstractly, which is to say, philosophically, and most indeed are. Different subjects will have greater or lesser call for the tools of one branch of philosophy over another; philosophers of mathematics will rely heavily on the machinery of formal philosophical logic in contrast to their need for ethical theory. Philosophers of psychology will apply theories propounded by philosophers of the mind and from the metaphysics of cognition, as will researchers in the fundamentals of artificial intelligence, complexity theory, network and systems theory and neuro-science. Philosophers of art will apply techniques honed in the branch of philosophy known as aesthetics and almost certainly those of epistemology (knowledge theory) will be applicable, perception being critical to art and epistemology alike. The political philosopher will be versed in many areas; logic, metaphysics and ethics in particular. The general techniques of philosophical enquiry will be employed in all such cases, namely tenacious questioning and a demand for utmost clarity of thought.

8.

Let us re-cap briefly before the relevance of these observations to financial markets is posited. Overwhelmingly, human conduct is carried out intuitively, habitually or by convention and this is a perfectly reasonable way to live. We handle the complexity of the world by shortcuts and approximations. Our decisions are often snap or *ad hoc* and the depth of analysis is shallow. Furthermore, this manner of conduct is *necessarily* abbreviated. If I am offered tea or coffee, I am ill-advised to think too deeply on the matter. The situation does not call for a metaphysical cogitation on the existence and nature of being of tea or coffee. Time spent dwelling on the ethical ramifications of choosing between a single cup of tea or coffee is unlikely to be time well spent in the grand scheme of things. We need not deliberate endlessly as to what we can truly know about tea or coffee. It is a simple matter of preference whose philosophical implications, if any, can be safely ignored to all practical intents and purposes.

But sooner or later in life more broadly complications do arise for which such cursory attention may prove inadequate. One might be confronted by an ethical dilemma whereby the appropriate action to take is not immediately obvious but nor indeed is the standard by which alternative courses ought to be judged. It is in just such cases that our thinking is likely to need to be of a higher order. The simple, parsimonious strategies for dealing with the normal ebb and flow of life are rendered insufficient in the face of situations that challenge the conceptual apparatus that convention and history have bequeathed us.

This is not merely true (although it is quite obviously so) in cases of moral uncertainty. When debate is concerned with the morality of a given action it is obvious that the conversation is philosophical by default. But other situations too can quickly require philosophical clarification. The discounting of modern art as not-art is one example.[4] The pro-life, anti-abortionist relies upon a particular reading of the ontology of persons; their concept of personhood requires a sophistication of meaning such that can encompass the foetus. A tell-tale sign that the conversation has taken a philosophical turn is the use of "But how do you define…" or "But what do you mean by…" In such cases, the issue at stake is not immediately resolvable and it seems a natural progression to examine the very meaning of the language and concepts in use. The reasons for so doing are manifold. It could simply be the case that the parties at loggerheads attach different meaning to the terms in use, in which case any agreement is likely to be merely coincidental and inauthentic; they are literally speaking on different matters. So if the anti-abortionist declares the belief that all human life is sacred and inviolable, the pro-abortionist might wholeheartedly agree. The point being that "human life" is conceptually too vague to draw out the distinction between the two (almost certainly) contrary positions. In the two earlier examples, the Magna Carta emerged when practical problems with the King's conduct and management style led to a fundamental review of the nature of Kingship, the rights of His Majesty's subjects and the responsibilities of the judiciary. In the case of Piergiorgio Welby, his request for his suffering, and in consequence his life, to end, (which to some without moral predisposition may not seem unreasonable given the most unnatural manner of his preservation and the very low quality of his existence) led to a thorough examination of the Italian laws pertaining to euthanasia. The assumptions upon which they rested were re-assessed.

Such difficulties arise not merely (to borrow the term from social science) at a micro-level, as in the case of individuals such as Welby.

On the macroscopic plane, dispute may arise between communities, socio-economic classes, religious or ethnic groupings or nations. In such instances the existing frameworks and procedures to attain a satisfactory resolution may well be adequate to the task. Negotiation may be possible on what might be called equal terms i.e. with the mutual presumption that the conceptual backdrop is jointly comprehended and identically formulated.

Despite this possibility however a situation of substantive complexity is unlikely to be durably improved by such elementary means. Human crises of great magnitude are almost invariably accompanied, if not preceded, by profound shifts in philosophical thinking. It is inconceivable to think the French Revolution could have been averted by some superficial, material economic settlement between the vested parties. The Revolution was inseparable from the concurrent thinking of the Enlightenment. The clash was not merely the economically advantaged versus the dispossessed; it was that of unsophisticated and outmoded thinking against a new revelation of man and his natural rights.

Confronted with a scenario that does not afford resolution by straightforward action, we are well served employing our reasoning faculties to make deeper inquiry. A richer comprehension of the situation is likely to lead to better decision making; it may not guarantee a successful outcome, but the limits of what can be achieved might be glimpsed, as should the standard by which we can judge our conclusions in time.

These claims should not be too controversial. To some they are doubtless almost too obvious to bother stating; commonsense pedantically expounded (a criticism regularly levelled at philosophy). Yet if this is the case, then the following claim should be all the more startling. It is suggested that the methodology outlined above is common to the vast majority of human experience and interaction. At the personal and societal level, we approach difficulties with pragmatism where possible but often turn the problem in on itself and question its nature more deeply, when a simplistic response seems insufficient. From how to conduct scientific work with rigour to how long one may reasonably detain suspected terrorists without charge, informal and formal philosophical techniques are employed to get to the heart of the matter. University scientific faculties offer courses in the philosophy of science. Faculties of law teach students jurisprudence, the philosophy of law. Political philosophy is routinely lectured upon, so intertwined are the two subjects. But the philosophy of finance is nowhere to be found.

Chapter 2

1.

This financial crisis has been remarkable in many ways. It has been a calamity of unprecedented magnitude, involving very recently evolved entities trading entirely newly constructed instruments in ways hitherto unimagined. The most simplified version of events, which applies to almost any credit crisis, tells of naïve creditors lending loosely to bad debtors and no doubt holds to some degree. Yet the greatest revelation of the crisis in the financial markets has been that this undoubtedly vital component of much of human society is entirely devoid of philosophical foundation. In consequence, the focus of debate as to what ought to be done has rarely looked beyond the immediate or considered much beyond what might be expeditious. A terrible shallowness to the discussion is inevitable given that no thorough contemplation of the subject's underpinnings has been undertaken.

Consider again how authorities and society have reacted to the crisis. Firstly, an attempt was made to prevent to complete financial collapse and this was entirely appropriate; one should not think languidly when emergency action is imperative.[5] But the actions thereafter have been a scrappy patchwork of dubious efforts at the margins to effect change or to give the appearance of decisiveness. Requisite Tier 1 capital ratios (i.e. the cash banks must hold as a fraction of lending) were increased, temporary restrictions on short selling were put in place, complex *ad hoc* restrictions on bonus payments were suggested, vague demands (or more precisely requests) that banks increase lending to firms were made, as were, in direct contradiction, calls for lending restrictions to be tightened. Enforced or encouraged mergers between retail and investment banks was an early tactic, despite denunciation of the concentrated, oligopolistic layout of the market as having compounded the problem in the first place and in spite of many asserting that banks ought to be 'broken up' and merchant/retail activities fully segregated.

It can be difficult to prove a negative hypothesis; to demonstrate that the field of finance has *no* recognisable philosophical basis. But the evidence for such a claim is considerable. There are no notable philosophers of finance in all of human history. The ethics of business have received some attention but the more specific ethics of say derivatives trading, as an academic pursuit, is unheard of. The philosophical meaning of the theory of capitalism has been extensively considered; but the meaning of capital markets, in terms of what exists, what can be known of them and how they ought to operate has received scant, if any, interest. If no formal proof of this deficiency can be offered, it is still hoped that the contrast between our approach to other matters of social and ethical complexity is so stark as to render the claim relatively uncontentious. At this juncture, as was the case in asserting that we are experiencing great difficulties with the financial markets, should there be passionate sentiment to the contrary, namely that there exists no such deficiency in our deep understanding of financial theory or that such knowledge is of no present or future value, persuasive evidence to this end must be offered. It is my suggestion that no systematic philosophical treatment of banking and financial practice has been undertaken, as we are now discovering to our cost.

Two questions follow from what has been claimed. Firstly, if we are in a spot of bother with regards to our financial markets and have not attempted to gain an insight into their true nature beforehand, what are the repercussions of our ignorance? And secondly, if we have considered most other subjects from the perspective of their philosophical founding principles, why has finance slipped through the net? Let us now consider the latter question.

2.

It is not hard to see why finance theory should have emanated from economics faculties in its genesis. Financial markets being in the set of all markets are clearly within the economist's remit. Indeed with their unique characteristics they often provide a paradigm case. Banks, hedge funds, proprietary trading firms are of course businesses which again brings them necessarily into the economist's focus. And clearly the entire financial system acts as a conduit for trade.[6] So the origins of finance theory are largely derivative of economic theory. As tends to happen in time with descendent or subsidiary subjects, its theorists have become highly specialised. The undergraduate study of finance has evolved from a brief mention as part of an economics degree, perhaps via courses on capital flows or market efficiency, into full length degrees in the subject. At the level of the Masters degree, the specialisation has become even more pronounced in recent years. When I studied for an MSc in Economics and Finance in the late 1990s, the choices were restricted to Economics and Finance, Finance, or perhaps Finance and Mathematics. The array of courses now available is astonishing and revealing: Master of Science in Mathematical Trading and Finance, Master of Science in Banking and International Finance, Master of Arts in Capital Markets, Master of Science in Audit and Financial Reporting are just a few examples.

This rapid evolution is driven in part by the accelerated growth in human knowledge. There are more academic researchers alive and working now, than in the rest of human history combined. The extraordinary improvements in network technology, microchip processing speeds and flow of information have clearly had an impact on the amount of knowledge humans can lay claim to. But the primary cause for the evolution of the courses on offer to their current specialised state is the demand from students. Students will seek the optimal return to their time and their financial investment (i.e. course fees) from their degree and presumably syllabus writers create content with this in mind. The students will understandably choose a course that they expect to maximise their attractiveness to financial institutions and so the course directors are guessing at what students are guessing the banks and hedge funds will look most favourably on.

As the sum of human knowledge expands, it seems inevitable that syllabi must abbreviate or specialise or do both unless courses are lengthened indefinitely. This is prohibited by the students' finite desire to remain students. So what tends to give way is depth, breadth and/or the seemingly inconsequential. If it cannot be put into a spreadsheet, it probably ought not to be taught, or so it would seem.

This approach will favour stochastic probability theory, econometrics, mathematical modelling and time series analysis. It will dispense with, not just the history of financial markets but also the history of finance theory. The philosophy of finance will obviously not be taught since the subject does not exist. The outcome of such a curriculum is a spreadsheet wizard who knows something about the efficient market hypothesis and weighted average capital, lots about statistical co-integration and virtually nothing about the market more broadly or practically. In my capacity as a senior trader I interviewed dozens of post-graduate finance students. In a rough experiment conducted only a decade after the demise of the hedge fund Long Term Capital Management (LTCM), I would ask interviewees what they knew of the firm. Only 30% claimed to know anything at all about LTCM, and fewer than that knew anything beside the name of the company. The collapse of LTCM is the most notorious hedge fund failure in financial market history. A combination of arrogance, ill-discipline, excessive leverage and an over-reliance on modelling techniques[7] led to the largest blow-up of a private trading firm in history. The fund was bailed out by a large number of the counterparties to its trades (banks) at a cost of several billion dollars. Perhaps comparative ignorance would be an MA political scientist unaware of the Berlin Wall, or an MSc particle physicist unacquainted with the Large Hadron Collider at Cern. The field of finance tolerates extraordinary degrees of historical ignorance.

This aside, it is non-contingently true that if the duration of courses does lengthen in direct proportion to the sum total human understanding of the subject (and this is clearly unfeasible) then specialisation or abbreviation is essential. And the casualties in such cases, where the re-numerative reward to study is imperative (as one might assert without excessive controversy that fewer students of finance theory are there for the love of the subject than in many other fields) will be those subjects whose *perceived* productive worth is least. History of the subject, history of intellectual thought in the subject and philosophy of the subject are perceived therefore as prime candidates for redundancy.

Yet there are far deeper reasons for the non-existence or under-representation of these areas in the modern finance curriculum. The dismissal of these aspects is not simply a recent phenomenon; it is a legacy of the subject's own early historical development.

3.

It is seemingly human nature to distil history into discrete and convenient narratives divided neatly into chapters. Perhaps this stems from the useful enumeration of time into month and years or from association of dramatic events with specific dates (1066,1492, 9/11)? Doubtless it has in no small measure to do with the expedience of simplifying that which is complex since our mental faculties are limited. Whatever the reason, one such simplifying assumption is that in 1776, Adam Smith fathered modern economic theory with the publication of his *Wealth of Nations*. Whilst Smith is now popularly remembered as an economist, he was certainly not viewed in that specialized light in his day. First and foremost, Smith was a renowned philosopher, and it was in this field this he contributed the majority of his work. Furthermore the economic ideas for which he is most fondly remembered such as the benefits of free trade and the division of labour are not original to him, regardless of his clarity of exposition. Smith was decidedly not the Einstein of economics.

His immediate influences were the great intellectuals of the Scottish and French Enlightenment movements, particularly Hume, Hutchison and a number of the so-called French Physiocrats. Although Smith lived as early industrialisation was gathering momentum, it is mistaken to suppose that economics only emerged from smoke; we can simplify the story only so far without foregoing important detail. We can assert however with greater confidence that at around the time of the publication of Smith's masterpiece of economics, the study of the subject *per se* was becoming distinctly recognisable and one can discern a spirit of enquiry that aims to be less normative and judgemental (as to how economies ought to work) and more objective, explanatory and descriptive in method than in previous eras. So for example in the economic ideas of the great British triumvirate of John Locke, Dudley North and William Petty (who between them, and a century before Smith, had written of the productive benefits of divided labour and the wealth creating potential of unrestricted trade), we find analysis not so much disinterestedly formulated for its own sake but more often to achieve some end. In Locke's case particularly, his economic thought is simply an adjunct to his political thought since his philosophical libertarianism required an account of ownership of worldly resources for completeness. This led to his fashioning a theory of how allocation and claims to (scarce) commodities could be legitimized and justified. His interest in the mechanisms by which allocation occurred (i.e. in what was known as political economy) was thus driven not so much by their properties and structures in themselves, but more by their incidental output and the philosophical connotations. Smith took the reverse approach. He decided in advance how and why people act as they do in his earlier work on 'moral sentiment'. And thereafter he described how such actions manifested themselves in the wider economy. This distinction marks an important point of division in the study of the subject; economics was emerging from philosophy, as the natural sciences had done earlier, as a standalone subject, interesting in its own right.

Dudley North (1641-1691), who successfully traded for many years in the Levant, wrote of the practical advantages of trade *per se* and the desirability of minimal state interference and regulation over 80 years before Smith published the Wealth of Nations. His analysis is more that of the man of commerce and action that that of Locke's high brow conceptualising. And he wrote with entirely practical intentions in the face of a turbulent political environment that he saw as threatening to commerce. His study of political economy therefore was not dispassionate or simply an ends in itself. Much the same may be said of the work of the third of the triumvirate, William Petty. His crude attempts at early econometric techniques (the measurement of economic phenomena) were but one practical outcome of his economic ideas, that were formed theoretically in intimate acquaintance with the work of the intellectual giants of the era, including Bacon, Descartes and Hobbes (to whom Petty was a personal secretary).

As one retreats in time, the economies themselves of course become more primitive and less comparable to those of later periods. And discussing contemporary economics as an academic endeavour becomes less and less meaningful. Thomas Aquinas, (c.1224-1274) was a monk and one of the greatest philosophers and thinkers of the medieval period. His economic thought is restricted to a handful of pages in the *Summa Theologica*, where he considers the notion of a 'fair' price, whether one may justly profit from trade and the ever-thorny matter of usury. The key point is that here the foremost thinker of his day is concerned almost exclusively with the *ethics* of trade and perhaps from a Dominican monk of the Middle Ages this is unsurprising. Aquinas is not an economist by any stretch of the definition. His outlook is entirely religious and his influences are the Scriptures and, as he calls Aristotle, 'the Philosopher'. From the perspective of the history of Western economic thought, the medieval period is a time of writers who are overwhelmingly Christian, considering only the ethical side of trade in an economy that was for the vast part agrarian. Where the outlook was not Christian, it was generally Aristotelian.

The economics of Aristotle, in his works that have survived, are largely confined to comments made in his *Politics* (which in itself is revealing). This far back in time however, some 2400 years ago, the structure of societies and economies are so wildly different from our own as to hardly sustain comparison. The Athenian economy of Aristotle's time was founded upon and sustained by a massive pool of slave labour. So whilst some of Aristotle's analysis can be made applicable (for example his distinction between trade of wealth for necessity's sake and for the simple accumulation of more wealth still has some validity), its real importance is preserved only by keeping the context in mind; this was a work concerning political philosophy first and foremost.

This historical diversion should serve to clarify Smith's real role in the history of economic thought. Even though, like many economic writers before him, Smith was primarily a philosopher, he was prepared to see economics as a matter of interest and importance in its own right. This was perhaps a more original idea than those of the merits of labour division and free trade.

Smith's work is also remembered fondly for the simple fact that much of what he wrote was correct. The reason for this is that he builds much of his theory on the assumption that the division of labour principle is true, as is undoubtedly the case. Indeed his advocating free trade is largely just an extension of the division of labour ideal. His famous example of the pin making factory whereby ten workers with modest tooling can produce 48,000 pins per day as opposed to just 10 per day were their labours not partitioned, makes an unarguable case for the principle. So much so that one might claim it to be an *axiom* of economics, i.e. self-evidently true and requiring no further demonstrable proof. Smith explains the three principle sources of the massive, exponential efficiency gain as i) the economies of time from the removal of the necessity to pick up and set down tools, ii) the opportunity afforded to the worker to practise and become highly skilled in a very particular task and finally iii) in the opportunity to create specialised tooling and plant for each task (which synthetically enhances the workers' dexterity).

So although Adam Smith was a philosopher, he is remembered as an economist. And the theoretical economists who followed were far keener to see themselves as men of science than of philosophy. Exceptions would follow to this rule, such as the highly political economic thinkers Marx and Bentham. Others would embrace the new discipline whilst maintaining strong links with the old, such as Mill and Keynes. But practising economists after Smith overwhelmingly attempted to re-cast themselves in a strictly scientific mould, with all that this entails. And the attraction of marching in this direction is obvious in hindsight; it was very much a case of joining the winning side as the efficacy and progress of science seemed unquestionable.

Following classicists such as Smith, Leon Walras (1834-1910) led the Marginalist movement that sought the full integration of economics into the scientific fold by the adoption of a single common currency and language; namely mathematics. The 18th century Physiocrats had likened economies to living biological systems and in particular they saw the subject anthropomorphically. Physiology was still founded on the theory of the Humours; the four chief fluids thought to constitute one's mental and physical being. Fine health was supposedly achieved by maintaining the delicate balance between the humours. In the ebb and flow of agricultural and industrial production and of the associated power wielded by land and capital owners, they saw a metaphoric living organism. It is no coincidence that Quesnay, intellectual head of the Physiocrats, was a physician before he turned his hand to economics.

But the Walrasians viewed economic systems less animatedly and less humanistically. If economics was to be a branch of any particular science, it would be physics and not biology. Walras saw economies as physical, dynamic systems and from this belief took his inspiration for their analysis from thermodynamics. This decision was to have far reaching consequences for the subject of economics for well over a century. From Walras, orthodoxy began to emerge that saw economies as systems that could be expected to find equilibria and throughout which economic 'energy' could be assumed to be conserved. Every facet of theoretical physics could then be brought to bear by assuming that economies were not merely analogous or akin to thermodynamic systems but were literal instances of them. Economics was to be a *part* of physics. A calculus was derived to approximate hard-to-measure parameters such as risk tolerance and satisfaction. Utility was the catch-all economic device for the philosophically tricky notions of desire and happiness. People looking for work to sustain themselves in spite of trying circumstances became agents offering labour units to maximise their utility (in units called utils) subject to external constraints. Codification in this manner allowed discourse of the subject to be conducted almost entirely in the language of mathematics. Not unlike the scientists of Newton's era who adopted Latin as the *lingua franca*, economists largely disavowed prose in the vernacular in favour of functional calculus.

The micro-economic, partial or localized systems theory of the 19th century, which had focussed on certain markets or particular types of agents, gave way in the early 20th century to grander, macroeconomic general theories. These vast aggregations of individual actions and a full generalization of lower-level assumptions were the output of men such as Marshall, Hicks, Samuelson and Arrow. The models were still predicated on long run equilibrium and it is therefore unsurprising that they forecast much the same. Markets should clear, imbalances self-rectify through price mechanisms and capital should flow from unrewarding persons and situations to the profitable risk-taker and enterprise. Steady growth should thus follow.

Naturally this methodology was not universally accepted and nor were the resulting models unanimously welcomed. Not only did some question the approach, they also remarked upon the awkward fact that these economists who thought themselves the equal of scientists and mathematicians were invariably to be found in Humanities faculties. It is undoubtedly a pity that these provocative comments were brushed aside and that a period of self-reflection did not take place. Instead, the agenda was firmly set by Milton Friedman's 1953 essay, '*The methodology of positive economics*'. In this work, he argues firmly against any normative or judgemental approach to the subject, and in some ways this marked the formal and final departure of mainstream economics from philosophy. He advocated the construction of objective models that simply forecast with maximal accuracy. One need give no account of oneself in the process; assumptions need be neither true nor realistic. No model need clarify the workings of the world. And those theories or systems with adequate predictive power should be ranked in turn by their simplicity on one hand and their fruitfulness (the lines of new inquiry they afford) on the other.

For an economist, Friedman was more philosophical than most; this essay draws heavily from the philosophy of science. Nevertheless, his assertions here are highly controversial. His emphatic insistence that predictive success outweighs explanatory power is not for the faint-hearted; afterall it is rare for scientists or engineers to be given such leeway. Ought a model forecasting that a bridge will not fail under duress, be accepted on the merit of previous such predictions as yet not contradicted by experience? Friedman rather too generously excuses economists from the requirement to *prove* any of those troublesome 'theories' or 'laws' that explain *why* something is the case. However he most emphatically does not encourage the adoption of blatantly erroneous assumptions, a criticism often levelled at the subject of economics. For this Friedman cannot be blamed. On the other hand he does firmly support the use of simplifying assumptions *per se*, and demands that enquiry is made into their effect upon the model's capacity to extrapolate effectively, should they be relaxed. Friedman's preference for simpler models (in contrast to say those of equal predictive power but greater complexity) has its roots in William of Occam and his fabled *razor*.[8] Whilst simplicity is arguably preferable to complexity, *ceteris paribus*, it is not an obvious or necessary virtue by itself. The world and human interaction therein is indubitably complex and unfussy explanation may be desirable but ultimately inadequate. As to the fruitfulness of a model, in terms of the subsequent lines of academic inquiry, whilst eminently desirable it is perhaps questionable whether this furnishes an hypothesis with such merit as to elevate it propitiously amongst the set of comparable proposals.

But let us not dwell overly on the detail of the arguments. For with the benefit of hindsight it becomes arguable that the importance of such an essay by Milton Friedman, emanating as it did from the University of Chicago in 1953, was magnified as greatly by the time and place of its publication as by its content. Few, if any, locations and eras have impacted upon the financial markets more, than Chicago in the mid to late 20th century.

Situated ideally as a nexus for trading the abundant mid-Western agricultural produce, the population had grown from a handful at its founding in 1833 to over 3.5 million by 1950. The Chicago Board of Trade was established as early as 1848 and with the exception of the Dojima Rice Exchange in Japan (where rice futures and forwards were trading in the early 1700s), the city pioneered the use of standardised exchange-traded futures contracts from 1864. The first exchange-traded stock options were printed at the Chicago Board Options Exchange on 26 April 1973. Today Chicago remains one of the world's leading financial centres.

The theory of finance was still in its infancy when Friedman wrote his book, *Essays in Positive Economics*. Over the next two decades, it would emerge as a field of study distinct from economics but inextricably descendent from it. Its early practitioners were generally economists, but occasionally converts from physics, statistics or mathematics. Few were historians or philosophers. It has become fashionable to disparage economists and financial theorists alike in the aftermath of the recent crisis. That is not the aim here. In some quarters not the slightest effort has been made to contain the glee at seeing 'genius fail' to borrow from Roger Lowenstein. A highly destructive mutual disregard seems to run in all directions; from scientists who sneer at economists and financial theorists, (barely it seems considering how advanced their own field would be were they all but unable to conduct any controlled experiments) and from the latter likewise in turn to traders in the dealing rooms (Nobel prize winner and Chicago finance theorist turned LTCM advisor Myron Scholes' infamous retort to an experienced derivatives trader who doubted the academic would be profitable, that he would because of "fools like you").

Of greater importance to this present analysis is not the detail of the finance theory that became orthodox, for better or worse. The minds that set about its devising were as brilliant and imaginative as any others and the denunciation of their output by academics from other disciplines and commentators at large seems to ignore both the immaturity of the field in question and the practical constraints of the matter; the laboratory is available only in the most limited sense to the economist and finance theorist. Furthermore, as pressing for our current purpose is the methodological inadequacy that finance theory has inherited from its parent subject economics. If the theory is mistaken, it is sound method that brings recognition of the fact and encourages subsequent rectification.

The path that finance theorists chose to tread amalgamated developments in the Chicago school of economics and the doctoral thesis of a largely forgotten French mathematician, Louis Bachelier (1870-1946). His PhD thesis, published in 1900, *"Theorie de la speculation"*, and its later resurrection, is one of those fascinating tales occasionally thrown up by the history of intellectual thought. Bachelier is an enigmatic figure. Neither his personality nor his insights seemed to conform; his character frequently hampered his academic career whilst to some extent masking the genuine originality of his ideas.

Even his subject matter was, at the time, off the wall; financial markets were hardly considered a fitting matter to detain the serious mathematician. Undeterred, Bachelier conducted the most serious study of the Paris bourse to date, where the bond market in particular was highly active along with associated derivatives contracts; futures, forwards and options. Aside from a taxonomy of the products being traded, Bachelier sought a way to marry the sound theories of mathematical statistics and probability with the seemingly chaotic and haphazard 'games' played daily at the Bourse. And this synthesis he achieved, by realising that it was highly improbable that one would ever know what would happen to say a particular bond's price because there was simply too much that was unknowable. The vagaries of politics, the hidden thoughts of all the market's participants, the likelihood of an earthquake: factors impossible to accurately account for or predict. But this is not the end of the matter; for it is similarly the case that one cannot *practically* know how particles will move when suspended in a fluid. And in this case, the application of probabilistic mathematics is all the more appropriate; since by knowing something about how particles move *on average* one can comfortably predict a *range* of outcomes with associated probabilities. In other words, one cannot predict what the price of bond X will be say six months from now, but by assuming the bond moves by *x* percent per day on average or that the daily change in the bond's prices follows a certain pattern or distribution, one can happily forecast a *range* of prices with certain probabilities that the bond will have in six month's time. The apparently random, yet understandable, motion of particles had been named Brownian motion (after botanist Robert Brown). Bachelier was the first to consider its application to the prices of financial instruments, which did indeed appear to be unpredictable and random. And with that, the paper was largely forgotten for half a century.

It resurfaced some time around the middle of the 20th century and was included in Paul Cootner's influential 1964 anthology

'The Random Character of Stock Market Prices'. Bachelier's stressing the importance of estimating a *distribution* of likely prices as opposed to the forecast of a single price, (which was the traditional approach taken by stock brokers and theoreticians alike), was still novel, and resonated with the contemporary feeling amongst academics that not only were these stock picking advisors unlikely in practice to significantly outperform their competitors (aside from the fortune good and bad luck afforded) but that it was, *ex ante*, theoretically impossible for them to do so. Beating the market by means of skill was not possible, *in principle*. In this light the best the investor could hope for was to optimise his portfolio with respect to his own risk tolerance. And minimise his transaction costs by sacking his broker.

It was with these assumptions embedded that now-orthodox finance theory began to be constructed. Modern Portfolio Theory (largely due to Harry Markowitz, another of the Chicago school) emerged in the 1950s advancing a method for asset allocation under the presumptions that stock prices moved like particles in fluids, all knowable information was already reflected in prices and that the only factor to truly consider was one's personal risk aversion. Eugene Fama, again of the Chicago school, developed the Efficient Market Hypothesis in the 1960s. This was a formal statement of Bachelier's idea that price movements could not be predicted precisely from the pool of available information. The hypothesis itself was to become a standard assumption in much, if not most, of finance theory for the rest of the 20th century. Another critical development in the theory, and one perhaps with the greatest and most enduring direct impact on financial markets in practice, was the model of Fischer Black and Merton Scholes published in 1973 to value option contracts. Building on the efficient market notion and Bachelier's application of Brownian motion to financial instrument price movements, they developed a closed-end solution (i.e. a relatively easy to calculate formula) to price option contracts that had hitherto traded on and off the official exchanges with only intuition and guesswork as the best guides to pricing. It is an extraordinary story that starts with an eccentric watching the Paris bourse in 1899, a paper forgotten for decades and its re-discovery directly leading to theories upon which hundreds of billions of dollars are traded globally on a daily basis little over a century later.

The line of thought that Bachelier had initiated, held sway for most of the second half of the 20th century. The starting point for most theorists was a set of simplifying assumptions that did not seem unreasonable. 'People act rationally to maximise their utility' is a paraphrasing of one such common assumption. It seems innocuous enough and has an immediate plausibility. People by and large seem to act sensibly and go about their business with a goal in mind that ultimately aims to increase their contentment. One works to earn a living to improve one's happiness. One spends leisure time pursuing activities that one enjoys. This is not obviously controversial. And assumptions to the contrary can seem highly doubtful at first glance: 'People act rationally to maximise their unhappiness' would be a bizarre starting point from which to try to model behaviour. The real weakness of the rational agent assumption is that it holds neither in perpetuity nor continuously. Sometimes people do act irrationally by whatever the set measure of rationality is thought to be. And sometimes large groups of people do this synchronously and for extended periods. As behavioural economists began to talk to behavioural psychologists they started to question whether the mathematical whizzes in the finance departments had simplified men's minds to a precarious extent for the sake of theoretical expedience. If human behaviour would only follow the neat little approximations that they wished to assume, centuries of theory developed in stochastic calculus, pure mathematics and even theoretical physics could be brought to bear. The prospects were just too mouth-watering for the theorists to ignore, and the assumptions were inserted, built upon and conveniently glossed over. Indeed, it is a wonder that students of finance theory wished to enter the City or work on Wall Street at all, having been endlessly taught that markets were efficient, that the work of traders, brokers and analysts was entirely futile with success and failure a matter of chance alone. Perhaps the continuing desire of students to enter the industry in spite of this propaganda suggests their intuitive response to the theory was that, at some level, it was plain wrong.

4.

So we may say that finance theory emerged in the mid 20th century, largely from university economics departments and of course in response to the innovations in the financial markets at the time. By this point, economics had been a stand-alone subject for the best part of two centuries and had attempted to align itself, after an early dalliance with biology, with physics and mathematics rather than with other social sciences. Political economy and the philosophy of economics took a back seat. Philosophers in general had all but dropped the subject. And finance theory was an offshoot of this algebraic version of economics. *As such, it had no notable philosophical consideration give to it.* The circumstances of its development were pushing the subject in this manner, whilst the market participants themselves lured the theorists to focus on unlocking the *profitable* potential of their trade as opposed to deeper questions as to its meaning and essence. The financial returns to individuals who could effectively develop practical applications out of the theoretical frameworks ahead of the competition could be astronomical. An arms race based on knowledge of financial theory began to occur. And a new threat emerged in consequence, (but was little remarked upon), namely that of the potential for catastrophe from the over-reliance on, or overly hasty implementation of techniques that were either imperfectly formulated or simply erroneous. The pecuniary returns to greater philosophical awareness of the markets are probably not immediately apparent to either market participants or society at large; it is generally the case that philosophy is greatly under-valued from the standpoint of its practical usefulness. Offered a scientist or a philosopher, the hedge fund or bank will likely not see any obvious selection dilemma; the scientist can be set to work, digging for opportunity in the mines of market data, whereas the philosopher is likely (some might suspect) to prevaricate incessantly and question every trading decision *ad nauseam*. Such, one suggests, is their perception. But whilst I would dispute this even in the case of individuals, at an aggregate level the returns to society and the markets generally of employing methods and persons overwhelmingly scientific and pragmatic and negligibly philosophical and concerned with abstraction, are undoubtedly sub-optimal. By allowing the market, and specifically the profit of financial institutions, to determine the methodologies employed, a skew necessarily exists towards that which is perceived to lead to immediate or short term profitability and away from that which may lead to overly-forensic questioning or bring seemingly unwelcome distractions to bear (such as matters of ethics, the greater good or the long run). It is not simply practitioners who are cast in this mould. The theorists both reflect and in turn propagate a system devoid of philosophical context. Regulators, who have spent decades in retreat, forever seem to take action in hindsight and without due foresight. Admittedly their role is unenviable, charged with policing some of the sharpest, most innovative and determined people on the planet whose pockets are deep and whose influence in the corridors of power is inestimable. The result is a depressingly *ad hoc* approach to the innovations of the market, a rules-based regulation on market activity that has a watery ethical basis borrowed from elsewhere without independent or original scrutiny, and an obvious tendency to be out-manoeuvred by traders and bankers. Their task is inherently difficult, but they surely do not help themselves by playing the part merely as passive administrators and bureaucrats rather than as proactive innovators in their own right.

The greatest cost and risk arising from this situation is borne of course, as we have recently seen, by society in general. As the financial markets have nominally grown in exponential fashion, so too have the potential rewards and risks. The recent crisis is but one in a succession of disasters that have upset the wider economy and despite the obvious trend for such scenarios to repeatedly occur, nothing has been done to plug the holes in the system. It is imperative that due philosophical and thoughtful enquiry, (as is conducted in almost every field of human intellectual interest), is given to all aspects of the financial markets because until such time, our understanding is condemned to remain shallow, our response to crises will always be spontaneous rather than sagacious, and the risk of total catastrophe will be unnecessarily elevated, or more troublingly, maximised.

5.

The preceding account argues that the discipline of the philosophy of finance does not appear to exist and that it is necessary to invent it. The source of its conspicuous absence is the historical disinterest shown by thinkers of all eras; from the philosophical snobs of antiquity who thought trade a base affair and whose own economies were built upon slavery, to the medieval ascetics defined entirely by their own religiosity and an ecclesiastical disposition that saw mercantilism as barely tolerable, to the Renaissance and Enlightened men who saw economics as but a branch of political philosophy, to the economists with allusions of scientific grandeur, to the finance professors chasing the quick theoretical buck as hungrily as any dealing room trader, to the modern analytic philosopher still considering ancient problems with ever-greater technical complexity and proudly professing utter ignorance of matters as prosaic and worldly as those of 'trade'.

It is proposed that in other areas affecting human existence, such deficiencies of insight do not exist and therefore when difficulties arise, a framework has been built that ensures some clarity of thought and avoids shallow, panicky and animalistic response. This is humanity in full expression of itself: considered, thoughtful, not infallible but with a capacity to learn and think laterally.

How then to begin to fill this void? How should one 'invent' the philosophy of finance? I suggest that this hitherto separate pair of businesses be subject to an enforced merger. This merger may bring something in the way of redundancies, (but hopefully only in so far as relates to awry theories), but also much in the way of synergy. Let the branches of philosophy shine their own lights on the world of finance; metaphysics, ethics, logic, epistemology, even aesthetics. And subject the components of the financial machinery to a full philosophical scrutiny. The process itself is likely to be as revealing as any tentative conclusions that are reached. Philosophy is generous in this way; and traders should recognise this as a rare example of a positive carry trade; one that pays its owner simply by virtue of being conducted.

Chapter 3

1.

Do financial derivatives contracts really exist? This question, one suspects, would be dismissed out of hand by professional philosophers and financiers alike, but for diametrically opposed reasons. The former group are likely to be repelled by the overly specific nature of the query; metaphysics (the study of existence) traditionally has loftier goals in mind such as what is meant by existence *per se*. When reference is made to actual worldly objects it is more often in so far as to prove a general point about the nature of being rather than to prove something about the precise object itself; a subtle distinction, but an important one. The financier, banker or trader is just as likely to be dismissive of the matter, but on a contrariwise account of its irritating abstractness. Surely there can be no literal profit from time invested in such consideration. And besides, the answer is blindingly obvious; of course they exist. Now go away.

Perhaps this prejudgment of philosophers and financiers alike is unmerited? It is after all necessarily suppositious since it is for a lack of evidence that due philosophical consideration has been given to such matters that I have asserted that there is a lack of interest in the task. And there is a sense in which this is fallacious argument.[9] But more troubling than any want of proof that answers have been offered to such questions is the want of proof that such questions have actually been posed. For now, as it is inessential to the argument, let us presume no reaction either way to my question but instead try to argue in favour of its merely meriting thoughtful consideration.

Philosophers do indeed focus upon much that is abstract. It is fair to say that they seek out abstraction. This seems to hold for all the philosophical sub-disciplines; so the theoretical ethicist for example will consider a specific scenario or dilemma, but at a deep level that aims to uncover the true, essential structure of the issue. They look to unearth that which is unique to the matter at hand and that which is indistinct from related cases. By digging down in this way, they aim to reveal the ultimate nature of the situation. And with such clarity, may come wisdom (optimally) or at least the next best thing, namely a subsidence of ignorance. The 'Do derivatives exist?' question invites abstraction and the consideration of something's proper essence. The answer is no more obvious than that of similar questions; 'Do I exist?', 'Does this table exist?' which have certainly come under the philosophers' radar. This subject matter therefore seems pre-conditionally perfectly acceptable fare for philosophical consumption.

As to why the financial market practitioner should trouble himself with such a question, I argue that such enquiry cannot realistically come at great cost (and actions with near zero downside are rare). Re-examination or (more likely in truth) examination of the most basic assumptions and tools of the trade will undoubtedly bring a certain clarity of mind and a keener awareness as to the limitations wrought by presumptions.

This chapter largely deals in what may be called issues within the metaphysics of financial markets. Metaphysics is not like particular branches of science, such as volcanology or human biology, which have large, but limited remits. Metaphysics, by definition, is at the root of most, if not all, philosophical discussion.[10] The major branches of philosophy overlap continually and any subject may be considered from each philosophical angle. However it seems expedient to consider certain aspects of the markets under the auspice of a single branch of philosophy rather than to consider each aspect of the markets from every philosophical angle at once. In other words, I am applying philosophy to the markets and will use the standard demarcation of the subject of philosophy as the road map.

And by necessity, I shall have to be selective. One cannot possibly hope for more than an introductory approach to the philosophy of finance, since it is as yet to even be introduced. Comparable subjects have a vast literature after decades or more of professional research. Instead we must content ourselves presently for a merely representative sample of what the field ought to encompass.

2.

Let us return to the matter of whether derivatives exist and re-phrase things a little to prevent anyone posing such a question being pelted from all sides with rotten fruit. A straightforward request, rather than to doubt existence *per se*, might be perhaps to be furnished with a definition of the term. And there is, in fact, a remarkable consistency across lexicographic sources that define derivatives, which tend to have something like the following structure.

Definition: A financial derivative is an f that derives its value from an underlying S.

For f one commonly finds 'financial instrument','asset','security' or 'contract'. For S one commonly may substitute 'security', 'asset', 'commodity' etc. This all seems relatively straightforward, on the face of it. But things often do before philosophers start raising irritating objections and asking how it is that one feels quite so sure of oneself.

This definition does two things. Firstly (i) it posits derivatives as a member of the set of all f s. A derivative is an f. Next, (ii) it gives a property of derivatives, specifically from whence they derive their value. Why do this? Well clearly (i) is an insufficient definition of derivatives, else the second term would be redundant and all derivatives would just be called f s. So the definition suggests that derivatives are f s with a certain additional, necessary property. It is not clear whether this property is unique to derivatives as such. In fact, this definition, which is given here in a generic but typical form and is pretty much an industry-standard, is in reality fairly hopeless, as any consideration of some real examples will show. Let us take a standard financial derivative, or rather to avoid begging the question, an object that is widely assumed to be a derivative by the financial community and show how this definition fails in practice. A futures contract is typically thought to be a derivative. It specifies the details of a trade which will happen at a specific, future date in accordance with certain market norms. A forward contract does the same but in a less standardized manner. The classic example (and probable actual origination of these contracts) is that of the farmer and the wholesale crop buyer. Before purchasing and sowing seed, it would be nice for the farmer to have some indication as to what price the crop will fetch at harvest. A forward contract gives him such certainty, subject to the risk that his counterparty may default or that his crop fails and he must then make delivery by buying the crop himself in the open market (and presumably at elevated prices if crops have failed generally), or else he must default with the accompanying damage to his reputation. He has exchanged one set of risks for another, as indeed has the counterparty to the forward contract, but he presumably did so willingly and he can then get on with simply being a farmer. A futures contract sets the terms in a standardised format that positively encourages a *secondary* market in futures contracts themselves to develop. So instead of Farmer A entering into a forward contract with wholesaler A that specifies a quantity of produce particular to Farmer A's tillable acreage, a futures contract has an industry-wide specification. On set dates a precise quantity of produce (say x tons or y lorry-loads) of a quality not below a known standard must be delivered. Farmers A and B may not be able to hedge away their risk precisely (in terms of quantity) using contracts such as these, but they will likely find the number of potential counterparties greatly increased, as the standardisation encourages re-trading and speculation.

Such are futures contracts. But are they derivatives as is widely believed? Let us accept that they are fs, in as much as we have allowed *f* to be fairly vague until now. If an *f* is a contract or a security or even an asset, it seems that a future qualifies as an *f*. This seems to lead to further questions, such is what is meant by a security or asset, but for now let us get to the heart of the definition, for we know that *f*-ness alone is an insufficient condition to classify something as a derivative. The fundamental, and here literally defining, property of derivatives is their derivation of value from elsewhere. In the case of a commodity futures contract, the obvious candidate for the so-called underlying S is the commodity itself. So, if a wheat futures contract is posited as a derivative, one might point to wheat as the underlying S from which the wheat future derives its value and hence its status as a derivative. Only cursory consideration however suffices to reveal this account's inadequacy. Certainly one might expect a relationship to exist between spot wheat prices (the 'underlying' product is often referred to as the 'spot' product and its price the 'spot price') and the price of wheat futures or possibly between their respective values[11], but there is a great deal more to say about a futures contract than this. The relationship between the spot price and the future price can be highly volatile. The liquidity in the futures market can grow to greatly exceed that of the spot market, such that the nominal worth of trading in the *derivative* market can vastly exceed the nominal worth of trading in the associated spot product. This seems to go somewhat against the grain of the standard definition. It is not uncommon for the derivative contract to appear to take on a life of its own and participants can trade effectively whilst paying scant attention to the spot market. At which point, can it really be said that all there is to the futures contract *qua* derivative is that it derives its value from the spot? When the perception of its value seems to be a confluence of a great many factors besides the spot value or price, to what extent does the definition still hold true?

The definition is creaking at the seams by this point, and a further problem, namely of feedback, is unlikely to help. The definition clearly denotes a feed-forward mechanism from spot value to futures; the reverse scenario is left unmentioned. And yet such feedback is commonplace in the financial markets. Whilst wishing to avoid unnecessarily esoteric examples from the markets, occasionally the importance of the philosophical point to be made will force the abstruse upon us.[12] A suitable example is the 'pinning' of a future's market around the strike of a particular option. An option is a derivative (or rather, to avoid begging the question, is widely perceived to be so) whose underlying product can be another derivative, typically a futures contract or a simple spot product such as a share or commodity. A simple option contract gives its owner the right, but crucially not the obligation, to trade a certain amount of the underlying product at a certain price (known as the strike price), on or before a certain date. Now options with different strike prices but identical expiry dates will simultaneously exist, and as the options on the future approach this time and date (typically monthly, but not essentially), it is not uncommon for the price of the futures market to gravitate to the strike of the option contract whose strike has the greatest open inventory. Open inventory is the outstanding inventory in the marketplace; if Smith and Jones trade 1000 lots between them, the open inventory is 1000. If Jones sells his 1000 lots on to Brown, the open inventory remains 1000. If Smith closes out his position with Brown, open inventory falls to zero. There are technical reasons why this pinning might occur[13] but more importantly this demonstrates an instance where the underlying product appears to be deriving its value from an associated derivative contract. This is in stark opposition to the suggested definition. Worse still, this circularity leads to an uncomfortable question as to the nature of the underlying product: when such feedback occurs does the spot product *become* a derivative?

From these perspectives, the typically used definition of a derivative certainly appears incomplete. It is not difficult to find financial contracts commonly accepted as derivatives that are inadequately classified by this prescription. Perhaps more worryingly, it seems to yield false-positive identifications: via the feedback pricing phenomenon, products traditionally considered pure spot must be classed as derivatives.

If the derivation of value of an f from an S is an insufficient condition to adequately analyze a derivative contract, what further properties might matter? One candidate is dependency. A spot product can exist in actuality and meaningfully without traders, banks and importantly, derivatives. A derivative however seems contingently existent and devoid of meaning without an extant underlying product. We can liken a derivatives contract on say an equity or Government bond to a bet between people on the result of a sporting contest. The existence of the game is independent of the bet, but the reverse is not the case; the bet has literally no meaning without the game.[14] Traders and risk managers happily offset all risks associated with spot and derivatives strictly by numbers. They will counterbalance directional risk (i.e. the risk due to the up and down movements of prices) between say a cash-equity and an index option (option on a stock index) and disregard any fundamental difference in the nature of the products. It is understandable that this simplifying assumption is made; it appears to hold for a great deal of the time and vastly increases the scope of possible operations. To ignore the close similarity between spot and derivative products, in terms of many of the features they exhibit, would make simultaneous trading of the products actually hazardous. For example buying coffee and selling short-term coffee futures, other things being equal, probably does have a netting effect that means directional price risk is reduced. To wilfully ignore this because one senses that the coffee beans and coffee futures are in essence different is as foolish as to trade them under the misapprehension that they are perfectly identical at heart.

This may seem intractable and therefore something we just have to live with. And yet in the recent crisis we have seen all too readily that physical existence, or at least an existence not predicated on the credibility or the continued survival of a counterparty, can have massive relative value in comparison to a contingently existent derivatives contract. For years leading up to the crisis, products were created that synthetically replicated physical products but at a fraction of the cost. These were essentially old-fashioned promissory notes whose prices simply reflected the prices of the physical products they simulated, with negligible account made for the likelihood of default. These 'derivatives' tracked the underlying physical spot products almost perfectly for years, until, in certain cases, the underwriter ceased to exist and the notes became instantaneously worthless. Until confidence started to wane in the credibility of virtually all counterparties globally, derivatives and spot had been treated with complete ontological parity. But in a crisis it is the *disparity* between the fundamental natures of spot and derivatives that comes to the fore. Sadly, this effect is like that of a smoke alarm that only functions in a smokeless environment. It seems one may safely assume that derivatives and spot share a great many fundamental properties, but that this assumption no longer holds when one truly needs it to.

However, even a property of dependency still does not sufficiently delineate spot products from derivatives. One need only consider the very first explicit financial market, namely the sovereign bond market, to see the distinction again go awry. Whereas a gold futures contract is dependent upon physical gold to have meaning, physical gold has no such contingent existence. The same case cannot be made however for government bond derivatives and the corresponding underlying government debt. Nation states come and go, governments fall, revolutions occur and the associated bonds can vanish without trace. Gold, on the other hand, has two essential properties; its supply is limited and it exists in perpetuity. If every nation state and financial institution failed tomorrow, not an ounce of gold would cease to exist. The same cannot be said of sovereign bonds.

Philosophical analysis is often divided into the normative and the explanatory.[15] The difference being that the former suggests how things ought to be, the latter simply how they truly are. An ethical judgement will usually be of the normative variety; 'murder *ought* to be thought immoral'. Our current consideration as to the nature of derivatives is an attempt at explanatory analysis, as metaphysical investigations tend to be. And in attempting to define or explain some phenomenon or other, philosophical analysis often looks for necessary and/or sufficient conditions that make for an adequate characterisation of the matter at hand. Our simple earlier definition of a derivative offers one such analysis; recall a derivative was posited as an *f* deriving its value from an underlying *S*. Here being an *f* is a necessary, but insufficient, condition, as is the property of 'deriving value from elsewhere'. The two conditions are independently necessary and *jointly* sufficient to define a derivative, under this analysis. These conditions provide a formal analysis of the meaning of the term 'derivative' which, it has been argued, is inadequate and inconsistent.

Philosophy has other tools in the box however to help with definition. One such method is that of *functional* definition. This involves replacing an arbitrary set of necessary and sufficient conditions by an attempt to define by virtue of an object's function. Examples are easy to come by simply by considering something best explained by reference to its function; a hammer, an examination, a computer programme. Currently derivatives are considered almost universally by some variant of the earlier definition and by this reckoning something either is, or is not, a derivative. Yet we have seen that this can fail in practice, for several reasons. Perhaps a functional definition therefore is more appropriate and helpful?

So can derivatives be understood functionally? Can we construct a robust and thorough description beginning with "A derivative is for…"? I suspect great difficulties will also confront this method. In trying to isolate derivatives from spot or other financial phenomena *by function*, the inherent flexibility and malleability of derivatives (which no doubt in part explains their extraordinary popularity) will work against us. The most junior of derivative traders should be able to demonstrate that derivatives may be re-arranged and combined such as to synthetically morph into a replica of any other derivative or spot portfolio, *in terms of function*. So, using futures and options on say sugar and a handful of interest rate swaps, it is possible to create a portfolio which replicates the *function* of a spot portfolio in sugar. True, it is a synthetic replication and many of the properties (such as exposure to counterparty risk) are non-identical. But the essential functioning can be so close as to make a distinction by function alone (which is the aim of this type of analysis) a realistic impossibility. In non-tangibles, perhaps a share instead of a commodity, the replication is likely to be even closer and indeed often by holding the derivative position until they expire, the match becomes literally identical, as derivatives can expire into physical holdings.

In short I am far from convinced that a functional analysis will prove fruitful. The function of derivatives is rather slippery by design and any definition based thereon has this to contend with. Similar problems are encountered if one casts the net wider to a categorisation of those employing these functional devices. A functional definition of the sort 'a derivative is an f used for purpose p' is suspect (since other types of f, and of particular concern would be underlying spot products, may be used for purpose p and hence become inseparable from 'derivatives'). But a definition invoking users such as 'a derivative is an f used by x' where x might be speculators or hedgers, which one might call a pseudo-functional definition, fails on the same grounds; namely speculator x might be able to use spot product f for the very same purpose and we are back to labelling spot as derivative, which is assuredly not *quod erat demonstrandum*. Is it possible that these attempts to define are failing for a reason?

It is entirely possible that this is the case. Derivatives, in essence, could be something far more conceptually abstract than financial market participants currently care to admit. And this is rather inconvenient since derivatives are thought to be well understood and perfectly definable. Banks after all have 'derivatives desks' and 'derivatives traders' and 'derivatives portfolios'. Risk departments believe that they know how to aggregate and offset exposures between cash books, bond portfolios, foreign exchange and derivatives. In short, products are considered distinct in this regard and the key distinction is derivative versus non-derivative. But this could be gravely mistaken, if derivatives ought to be considered not so much as a product set but as a concept. Derivativeness might be more apposite than derivative.

A useful simile might be property. What is the meaning of the term property? Perhaps surprisingly, this has occupied philosophers and law-makers alike at length. The notion of property has a prominent place in political theories, the philosophy of rights and obvious legal implications in practice. One insight that such research has to offer is to suggest that property ought to be viewed conceptually. Property can be thought to consist of a series of rights and powers over objects. Being able to classify objects as someone's property depends not on some inherent feature of the object itself but by virtue of what the concept of property entails.

So it may be with derivativeness. An instrument or object is not a derivative by nature, but in consequence of what the concept of derivativeness means. So when a futures contract begins to drive a spot market, we can see the spot market is conceptually in some way derivative. And the futures contract furthermore in so acting in this respect is not behaving derivatively. A series of such incidents of derivativeness could be envisioned that would serve to expound the concept. Then, as the concept of property permits a considered judgement to be made as to where ownership truly rests, it may be possible to classify instruments into spot or derivative. But the results certainly may not match our current expectations.

Does this mean that the original definition was in some ways valid, since it did seem to indicate that a spot product could in fact be considered a derivative, which is akin to the insight just posited? Well, not quite, because it attempts a delineation that is stricter than seems necessary. The spot product being driven by its own associated futures market is a *de facto* derivative by this definition. But by viewing derivativeness as a conceptual term we can state perhaps with greater accuracy that the spot product has a derivative element or that it exhibits some partial derivativeness. In effect, there may be far more to the term derivative than the simple qualification of a noun which the original definition attempted.

The implications from this line of thinking are profound. The *status quo* is a universal presumption across the financial markets that derivatives are clearly defined and classified, by law and for all practical purposes. I hope that this elementary inquiry casts doubt on such assertions. The true nature of derivatives is surprisingly elusive, which makes the trillions of dollars staked on their existence on a daily basis disquieting. Regulators and financiers alike operate in this arena as though the fundamental questions have all been posed and the answers fully digested, and that it is merely a matter of tinkering at the periphery and calling this activity 'market supervision'.

After a decade of trading derivatives, I was left certain of two things. Firstly, that they are extraordinarily powerful. Einstein famously identified compound interest as the most powerful force in the Universe, but derivatives have an in-built non-linearity and exponential aggressiveness that makes compound interest seem more like simple interest in comparison. Secondly, although I felt I knew how to handle the derivatives books I managed, with hindsight it was in the manner of a driver having very little idea not so much of how a combustion engine works but of what is truly meant by 'a car'. And having hopefully demonstrated the inadequacy of standard definitions and the difficulty that other philosophical techniques might also have in providing answers to the question 'What is a derivative?', perhaps it is less clear now that the metaphysical question 'Do derivatives exist?' is as whimsical as first appearances might have suggested.

One final note on this matter that suggests philosophers and derivative traders were not always so far removed from one another. According to an account given by Aristotle in his *Politics*, Thales of

Miletus, widely regarded as the first ever recognisable philosopher, was no mean trader himself of products that look decidedly derivative. By allegedly forecasting the weather with accuracy, Thales foresaw a bountiful olive harvest. Early in the season, he paid deposits to secure the hire of every olive-press in Miletus and nearby Chios, thus creating a squeeze in the price of presses when the time came. Thales then could name his price.

"When the season came, and there was a sudden and simultaneous demand for a number of presses, he let out the stock he had collected at any rate he chose to fix; and making a considerable fortune he succeeded in proving that it is easy for philosophers to become rich if they so desire, though it is not the business which they are really about."[16]

3.

It is commonplace for investors and traders to be presented with information of the following sort.

What the brokers say about fictitious company ABC

Current shareprice: $1.30

Broker	Recommendation	Target Price
Stanley Goldberg	Buy	$1.45
Banque de Blanc	Strong Buy	$1.80
Fiduciary Broking	Hold	$1.35
Greenfeld and Co	Strong Sell	$0.80

Although names are fictitious and the currency has been altered, the actual data was perfectly true and pertained to one of the largest telecommunications companies in the world. An entire sub-industry within finance is devoted to the publication of such material; partly as a genuine attempt at a value-adding advisory service to clients, but assuredly no less as a marketing device. Altering a recommendation or target price for a stock might garner ten seconds of attention on the numerous business channels who have long schedules to fill. And bear in mind that brokers' commissions on their clients' trading activity is invariable to the direction of trade. In other words, the brokerage house's primary concern is that the client should trade, not that he should trade in the direction that they think is likely to be profitable. Naturally they make claim to the contrary; that their long term interest is best served by the client making good trades and being profitable himself in the longer term. But the strength of this conviction rarely, if ever, is such that they refuse to execute trades on a client's behalf that they firmly believe contrary to his best interest.

Such data is so common a feature of the markets that one seldom ponders too deeply on it. And yet, in so doing, one uncovers a philosophical problem that lies very much at the heart of practically all trading that occurs in the financial markets. To see this, let us formalize the above example and suggest the assumptions upon which it might be thought to rely.

Each broker has knowledge of the price of the stock, ABC. Let us call this price, p. This is publicly available and presumably uncontroversial. Each broker then makes a pronouncement as to whether this p is greater than or less than the stock's value, which we shall call v. So we might have something like this:

Broker	p vs v	Assessment	Recommendation
Broker A	$p>v$	Over-valuation	SELL
Broker B	$p<v$	Under-valuation	BUY
Broker C	$p=v$	Fair value	NEUTRAL

This is the system at its simplest. In practice, gradations of columns thee and four have evolved, depending largely on the magnitude of the difference between p and v. So if p wildly exceeds v, the recommendation might be STRONG SELL or a p marginally less than v might attract a HOLD or ACCUMULATE rating rather than BUY or STRONG BUY. The definitions of these recommendations are not truly standardised and vary from broker to broker.[17] Now the obvious line of questioning needs directing towards v. What precisely is meant by the 'value'? What is its nature and how and what can be known of it? The brokers seem confident not only that they know what value means, but that they can attach a precise number to it. We can infer that value is believed to be enumerable since it is presented comparatively to price, itself a number.

It appears that the brokers believe that the stock, or perhaps more accurately the company of which the stock constitutes a share, has a value. In this regard it is not uncommon to hear reference made to the 'true, underlying value' of an asset. But what exactly does this mean? What is this value predicated on and what is the nature of the relationship between this value and the price of assets? It is doubtful there is a more relevant philosophical field of investigation than this to the financial markets.

A typical response to the question of what is meant by value is to make an appeal to the notion of 'worth'. Value is 'what something is worth'. Aside from verging on the tautological, there are other problems with this reply. For as many a trainee trader is taught, to truly discover what something is worth, one simply enquires as to what someone is prepared to pay for it. But this has the effect of equating value to worth and worth to the market price, which by transitivity[18] implies value is merely the same as price i.e. $v=p$. This result contradicts the brokers who certainly do not profess to believe that parity holds between price and value. And a contradictory outcome often points to faulty reasoning or premises. Perhaps then value is indeed worth but this is not necessarily equal to the bid price in the market? But this does appear simply tautological and little has been resolved.

The logical Law of Non-contradiction tells us that not all the brokers in tables one and two can simultaneously be correct. The statement '$p>v$ and $p<v$' is a logically false statement. Presumably v is furthermore publicly unavailable in the same manner as p else all brokers would agree in their comparison. This much we can safely ascertain.

So we have inferred that brokers believe stocks to have a single, true value which is enumerable. They must also believe that a dependable relationship exists between price and value, since they make recommendations on how to trade the stock based on the difference between value and price. Perhaps there is something to be gleaned as relates to value by investigating the nature of its relationship with price?

In making recommendation to trade based on the p,v differential, the broker seems to suggest that there exists an imbalance between p and v which should in time be righted. Furthermore, the broker must believe that it is the price that will be revised to meet the true valuation rather than the value that moves towards the price. This is obviously his reasoning, since if he thought the value would move and the price be static, he would have no grounds to recommend trading the stock one way or the other. No broker seems to believe that the stock is presently under-priced ($p<v$) but that the valuation v will fall to rectify the imbalance.

The assumption seems to be that the nature of the relationship between price and value is one of correspondence. There is a belief that the price should correspond with the valuation and that where it does not, the price, and not the valuation, will move to restore some sense of parity or equilibrium. This thinking, we have met before in discussing equilibrium based economics; a creed that expects markets to clear in the long run, equilibria to win out and imbalances to self-rectify via price mechanisms. Now if this belief is held, one might perceive the endless volatility of stocks and assets and ask precisely when this 'long run' will take shape, for surely once $p=v$ the speculative reasons for trading vanish and any trading that does occur must be simply to rebalance portfolios. Can this story be believed when there is a want of any obvious such occurrence in the markets; of prices settling down to match genuine valuations?

The obvious caveat is to deny that value is a constant. For p to equal v may be a simple result of happenstance. The only real constant in the markets is change itself and a multitude of factors, themselves endlessly altering, will serve to affect the value of the stock. Nevertheless, the broker must believe that the valuation will be static enough to be relied upon for trading purposes. He recommends our trading on his advice because he sees the price, claims to know the value, and believes price will adjust to value and not *vice versa*. Given this, we should be able to put the broker to the test over time, by following his advice and tracking our profit and loss. Would this prove that his account of the relationship between value and price is correct? Of course it would not. There could be many other reasons why we make or lose money by following the broker's tips, none of which require the belief in the price-value correspondence idea to be true. Sadly, the hypothesis cannot be isolated and tested in this manner, although with a degree of cynicism one might not expect the broker to lose sleep over this experiment's implausibility.

Why should price move towards the true value? Well presumably if the price consistently reflected the incorrect value, the asset in question could be held profitably in perpetuity. So if say a stock is priced at 10 pence and the company has paid a 50 pence annual dividend for the last 100 years, one might expect the price to be driven up, since anyone buying the stock at 10 pence will have their investment re-paid five times over after just one dividend payment and thereafter collect a risk free income. This situation cannot, realistically, go on indefinitely in a free and open market, as buyers will be prepared to pay more and more for the asset, driving up the price. So in this case, we are suggesting that the value was far in excess of the reflection in the current price, that investors will recognise this in time and gradually the price will increase to better mirror the valuation. This all seems intuitively reasonable. The valuation is some function of the income stream emanating from the asset and indeed this is a common starting point for models that aim to value assets. Value is determined by some measure relating to the discounted income stream. It is often claimed that an asset should be worth the income it will yield over the period it is held, discounted by the time value of money.[19] Here then is probably the most widely accepted conception of value in the financial markets. But is this the true meaning of value or simply another means of approximating it? And does any such difference matter?

There are many problems besides with this idea of value, probably the most compelling of which is that many assets considered valuable (i.e. to have value) do not yield any sort of income. The class of such assets is very large; crops, metals, zero coupon bonds and non-dividend paying stocks. It may be countered that these should not therefore be classed as genuine assets. This is as maybe; it does not affect their property of being perceived to have a value. In these, and therefore presumably in all cases, the factors that valuation seems to encapsulate are manifold and cannot merely be a function of income. When assertions are made by traders and brokers as to the under or over valuation of say industrial metals or of volatility based derivatives, which pay nothing to their owners, what then can they mean? We are no closer to understanding the nature of the value of an instrument.

Value seems to be something that every financial asset or product is presumed to have, whether income yielding or not. It is assumed to be enumerable and also therefore that an estimator of the value can be formulated. Typically this estimator is the output of a model that tries to capture the essential factors that contribute to the value. Now the true value, presuming that it exists, would be the output of a perfect model. This model would have to include everything that will happen in the future that will affect the asset or the company etc. Very quickly, this must escalate out of all comprehensible proportion. A perfect model must include the contribution of the Chief Executive to performance, the fact that he will drop dead from heart failure in three month's time, the as yet un-made decision of a major customer to increase its regular order by fifteen percent, the as yet un-made discovery by the worker in a competitor's R&D department that will halve their production cost etc. etc. This may then appear as a sarcastic swipe at the ambition of analysts who try to estimate value by modelling techniques. But in reality their models are massive simplifications and estimators aiming to capture just something of the preceding possibilities. The perfect model cannot be built with all the will or supercomputing power in the world; it is little less than a Laplacean demon.[20] But can a necessarily parsed model be constructed that retains adequate detail to furnish its creator with a sound estimator of value? We must conclude that brokers do believe this to be the case; that the true value might be a function of a near infinite array of un-knowable factors but that a sufficient proxy array can be fruitfully employed.

This result is continually over-looked in the financial industry. Note how the original broker recommendations did not specify that the relation between price and value was anything other than objective. Their recommendation is of course derived from their subjective opinion, but the claim seems to be that the price is mis-marked relative to the true *objective* value. This assumes that such a value exists in the first instance, but also that their estimator of value is the product of an extremely good model. Why is this remarkable, one might ask? What is noteworthy in stating that different brokers use different models and have different valuations? It is important because the distinction between the *objective* value and the *subjective* value is almost entirely over-looked, confused or forgotten, with serious consequences.

For example, a great deal has been made of the weaknesses of mark-to-market accounting before and during the recent crisis; indeed some commentators have posited this as a *primary* cause of the subsequent problems following the collapse in the sub-prime real estate markets. The hypothesis is that marking assets to market (i.e. placing a valuation upon them equivalent to the market price, namely setting $v=p$) led to distortions in portfolio valuations because firstly banks and other institutions were bidding-up (i.e. 'artificially' elevating) prices to protect asset valuations, and secondly when the liquidity evaporated from the market, valuations, which were simply recorded as a direct function of price, became too inaccurate. The main alternative valuation method to 'marking to market' is fair value accounting. This is the use of modelling techniques to estimate values. Now one reason one might suspect that this latter idea has support currently is the belief that true, objective value a) exists and b) is largely knowable with a sufficiently robust model. But the aforementioned result is all too easily forgotten. A model gives a subjective *impression* of the value and not necessarily the true value itself.

A useful metaphor for this limitation is found in the metaphysics of Immanuel Kant. He of course was dealing with the existence of reality in its entirety; it is doubtful he was motivated by problems regarding sub-prime derivative valuation. Nevertheless, his conclusion was that we can have no access to reality. We have an inescapable cognitive set-up such that we can only observe our *perception* of reality. Many of the standard metaphysical questions for Kant, such as whether God exist, whether we can have free will or what is meant by personal identity, were not quite meaningless but certainly did not have the objective answerability we might desire or expect. We simply cannot escape our perspective of reality in order to access the objective truth.

Relating this Kantian sentiment to the brokers in the financial markets (which is, one suspects, a first), true knowledge of valuation could well be not merely practically unattainable but *a priori* theoretically inaccessible. Too much is unknowable and models might be inherently blinkered with regards to value, much as our own perception is to reality. For Kant, this left room for faith; in God, free will and existence generally. But bankers all too often forget that their trading in assets because they are 'mis-valued' is *an act of faith*. Their valuation is a subjective impression of what is quite likely an unknowable or even non-existent true objective value. Nothing more. Yet how often one has heard traders claim to 'know' something's true value. "Sterling is 22% over-valued". "Collateralised debt obligations were 8% under-valued". Substituting certainty for faith in models and spreadsheets is wildly dangerous when done in ignorance of the fact. As we have learnt however it seems a near inevitable outcome when vast capital commitments meet egoism.

Discrepancy in perceived value is at the root of all trading in financial instruments. And yet it is not clear that a deep understanding of the meaning of value, nor its supposed relation to price, exists in any convincing form. It is just such ignorance that led to rival banks paying bonuses to *all* traders on competing desks, on the strength of positions that were equal and opposite in terms of inventory, but whose profitability was 'valued' according to the traders' own models. Bank A would pay a bonus to Trader A on the *theoretical* profit from his position measured against his own valuation, whilst Bank B would pay a bonus to Trader B on the equal and opposite position since he too registered a profit but using *his* own valuation (which of course was different to Trader A's). The profits and losses from this trading must necessarily sum to zero and both traders' valuations cannot be correct. Eventually, and probably long after the traders have jumped ship, at least one of the banks will realise a loss on the position, against which they have already paid out a bonus, compounding the problem. I have even observed in this precise situation the losing bank, say Bank B, sack Trader B and pay a very large "golden hello" to Trader A from Bank A to come and clean up the mess; after all he knows the position already, since he was managing the mirror image portfolio. Of course this leaves Bank A with a large and now unmanaged position. Luckily for them, there is a trader available in the market who knows precisely how to handle the position and a head-hunter, for a large fee, will secure them the services of "expert" Trader B. I saw this fiasco played out on several occasions in the lead up to 2008, even to the extent that hypothetical Trader B would *return* to Bank B and Trader A to Bank A, again for large guarantees. It is little wonder that banks had nothing set aside to cover losses when theoretical valuations proved erroneous on a massive scale; successive and inappropriate bonus payments had acted as attrition in this manner for years.

4.

One wonders what credence the Bohemian preacher Jan Hus gave to the guarantee of safe passage promised by the Holy Roman Emperor, Sigismund, as he set out for the Council of Constance, Germany, in late 1414. He placed his trust in the Emperor and no doubt in God Himself; but nevertheless reportedly took the precaution of drawing up his will before departing. The Council had been summoned in an attempt to end the Great Schism then affecting the Roman Catholic Church, which had resulted in the somewhat preposterous situation of having three separate claimants to the papal seat (Pope Benedict XIII of Avignon, Pope John XXIII of Rome and Pope Gregory XII of no fixed abode but usually somewhere in Italy). Besides deciding on a single pontiff, the Council aspired to settle the grievances of malcontents such as Hus. He had been charged with the old theological chestnut of heresy. He had spoken out against ecclesiastical and papal practises such as the ever-profitable sale of indulgences and, as he saw it, an excessive alacrity for engaging in warfare. In this light Hus was a direct ideological forebear of Martin Luther and the Protestant Reformation. In fact, Hus' ideas and writings were largely borrowed, or directly plagiarised in many cases, from those of Englishman John Wycliff (c.1325-1384). Wycliff had also been deemed heretical, but only suffered physically for his 'crimes' a considerable time, one suspects, after he had ceased to care; in 1428, at the behest of Pope Martin V his remains were exhumed and burnt. Hus was not to be so fortunate. The indemnity promised by Sigismund proved worthless and the dissenter was burnt at the stake in 1415.

Also in attendance at the conference, (which incidentally was probably the greatest networking event of the late medieval period and as a direct consequence of which alliances and commercial links were established that lasted for many decades thereafter), was one Cosimo de'Medici, son of Giovanni di Bicci and heir to the great Medici Bank. His interest in proceedings was less in doctrinal matters than in the decision regarding the appointment to the top job. The Medici had backed John XXIII to the tune of 95,000 florins, a vast sum in its time. The monies had bought off King Ladislas of Naples who previously had supported Gregory XII and had waged war on John's Papal States. The Medici however, with greater foresight or perhaps less appetite for self-destruction than Jan Hus, had requested more than fine words as security. John XXIII put up a jewelled mitre and raided the Papal vault for gold vessels to collateralise his debt.

The Medici bet on the wrong horse. John was accused, as 18th century historian Edward Gibbon memorably records, 'of piracy, murder, rape, sodomy and incest', and yet, 'the most scandalous charges were suppressed'. Wisely sensing the game was up, John absconded before the trial went into too much grisly detail. He still aimed to play his last and potentially trump card, namely that the Church council became ecumenically null and void without a Pope to chair it. Perhaps forgetting that the conference was awash with Popes, John's gambit failed and he was deposed *in absentia*. The other remaining Popes fared little better, as the Council voted 'none of the above' and decided to start afresh with a Pope Martin V. John was declared an Anti-Pope and erased from the official list of St Peter's descendants, leaving as a legacy a papal name so tainted it would be some 500 years before another Pope John XXIII came along.

These events, which the great stretch of time since elapsed renders somewhat quaint or faintly comical, were of course of utter seriousness in their day. They also contain important lessons and offer rich evidence for those interested in the question of what it is that makes a bank, a bank.

It is only too obvious why this question is of relevance. The role of banks in the recent crisis is unquestionably, (and perhaps a little too charitably), non-negligible. In many quarters the banks are blamed to the fullest possible extent for what occurred. But before blame may be apportioned, culpability correctly attributed or even exoneration bestowed, and before one looks to legislate so that banks are better regulated, it is of paramount importance to have, if not a working definition, then certainly a comprehensive understanding of what makes a bank, a bank. Proceeding in ignorance on this point renders success or failure of any regulatory action a matter of simple chance. I shall argue that traditional approaches to the problem have failed to capture the essential nature of banking and that this affords little prospect of effective regulation. It also hinders our capacity to understand how it is that banking crises recur so readily.

A typical answer to the question of what makes a bank, a bank is to offer a functional exposition as to common activities in which banks engage. But this rudimentary response is unlikely to be satisfactory. So, a bank collects deposits and makes loans at interest, facilitates the exchange of currency, invests depositors' funds, advises in financial matters, trades commercially for its own account etc. etc. Indeed some institutions normally deemed to be banks, do some or all of these things. But some specialise in one area whereas others do much more besides. There may be two institutions engaged in these fields but with no overlap between them. Where should the lines be drawn? Perhaps it is a matter of analysing these various functions more carefully and aiming to collate a set of essential criteria that allows for the formulation of strict definition? This in fact is very much the course that society has taken to date in understanding banking. It has been ramified time and again into sub-sections that approximately relate to function; retail banking, private banking, investment banking, central banking, clearing banking etc. But let us consider carefully from whence these categorisations draw their provenance.

We recognise that certain activities in the course of human societal and economic history have a financial element to them and it is with this that we most nearly associate banking. Whenever in history we find evidence of trade, industry, economic management, complex political organisational structures, we will tend to find some corresponding element of determined pecuniary effort. In the known history of human societies which lacked such advancement, such as the hunter-gather tribes-people of pre-history, we find a dearth of any activity which corresponds or resonates with any notion of banking, for the entirely obvious lack of want thereof. If we believe banking has something inextricably to do with money, trade and commerce, we should be concerned at its presence, in their absence.

Wherever and whenever we find evidence of substantive trade, be it of agricultural output in ancient Mesopotamia or of high-tech modern intangibles such as software, we find persons or groups of persons acting as *facilitators*. This facilitation service, at its most primitive, probably begins with ensuring a literal exchange of property is logistically feasible. Barter systems, the precursor to systems of currency or money, (and fall-back option when currencies implode) are a gross impediment to trade, economic growth and prosperity and so it was that coinage evolved. Now the facilitators of non-barter exchange, who deal with ensuring that monies and payments clear or with the appropriate exchange of one recognised currency for another, may, perhaps, be recognisable as bankers. They have established banks (physically and figuratively) for the specific purpose of conducting such business. And yet, the evidence is that activity of this sort was conducted in Temples long before a stand-alone banking network evolved.

The desire to acquire and trade resources that are scarce has, throughout history, often led to warfare. The ability to wage war rests on an ability to pay for it, although often the means and ends of warfare have been reversed. The Roman Empire is perhaps the paradigm for a self-financing territorial expansion, which sustained itself for many centuries. On the other hand, the Crusades were a far less successful attempt to make war pay for itself. Wars, and specifically their funding, have often created new financial markets, and since the inception of recognisable open exchange in financial instruments, few events have had a greater capacity to affect prices and trading. In the early 19th century, Nathan Rothschild's nascent bank profited by offering Wellington a reliable mechanism for securing payment to his troops (by the physical transfer of bullion) but later moved into speculation over the price of British sovereign debt as the Napoleonic wars played out. Here then we see what was essentially a logistical, operations company dealing with the clearance of payments, concurrently act as proprietary speculators. And this was certainly not the limit of Rothschild's dealings.

Before the nation states of recent centuries emerged, it can be more propitious to reference with respect to monarchies. And as a system of governance, monarchy has always required what appears to be banking functionality at its disposal. This was certainly the case under feudalism, when a peasantry literally had very little at the margins to pay in taxation and so ulterior sources of finance were necessary; banking operations of a sort arose to fulfil this need. Servicing the account of a King or Queen may have bestowed prestige upon the banking house or family in question, but the risks could be ruinously high. Edward III of England bankrupted the three leading Florentine banking dynasties following a depression in 1340 and the commencement of the 100 years War with France. His default to one of the families alone was thought to be for an amount equal in value to that of his entire realm.

This was an early example of fiduciary banking, an innovation, like many others that had its origin in 14th century Italy. Fiduciary loans were unsecured, with the debtor's word the sole guarantee to the creditor. In the case cited earlier of monies lent by the Medici to the rogue John XXIII, the Pope's creditworthiness or trustworthiness was insufficient for a loan to him to be purely set on fiduciary terms. Or else he presumably sought a lower rate of interest on the debt by offering collateral (the precious mitre and golden wares). The Papal account was similarly prestigious for banks to seek to secure, but with a risk profile somewhat different to that of a Royal household. The Vicar of Rome had revenue streams unavailable to monarchs, in particular the sale of Saintly relics, indulgences and Bishoprics or other seats of ecclesiastical office. By the late Middle Ages this business had become sizeable, with the printing press allowing 'indulgence inflation' to occur. Against these sources of income however, the vicissitudes of Papal succession and a frequently reckless profligacy exposed their bankers to risks that bloodline-successive monarchic accounts were in some ways insured against (since succession was, theoretically, assured). With these exposures to the typical banker's capital in mind, one might anticipate his attempting to influence political proceedings directly. And sure enough, as we find banking wherever there is commerce and war, monarchies, States and Papacies, we find bankers and financiers themselves rarely content to remain passive observers of the powers that be and to simply accept whatever fate befalls their investments. Instead they have tended to attempt to protect their stake-holding by exerting direct influence. When Machiavelli wrote his treatise on governance it was meant as an instruction manual to the man to whom it was dedicated, Lorenzo de'Medici, ruler of Florence. But note the title, *Il Principe*; the Prince. By the time it was written in 1513, the Medici had risen in little over a century from simple money changers to Royalty, in all but name. They had also provided two popes (Giulio de'Medici, Pope Clement VII and Giovanni de'Medici, Pope Leo X) and two queens of France would soon follow (Catherine and Marie). In more recent democratic times, the direct influence of bankers is via the two-way street of political donation on one hand and appointments to public office or favourably regulatory regimes on the other. Politicians often enjoy non-executive directorships on the boards of banks whilst City grandees enjoy peerages and knighthoods and Wall Street heavyweights can enjoy appointments to influential Treasury posts.

It is easy to become conspiratorial about such matters, but that is not the present intention. It is merely to edify that where one finds, throughout modern history, activity conducive to, or presenting opportunity for, banking practices, one often finds that the relationship between lender and debtor that is formalised by contract is also given informal reinforcement by a personal connectivity. Whether it is a Medici becoming a Pope or a former Prime Minister sitting on the board of an investment bank, this type of interconnectedness between brokers of power and brokers of finance is ubiquitous throughout time and place and simply reflects what appears to be an essential co-dependency.

We have so far considered some of the conditions that prevail to encourage banking activity, but how specifically do such enterprises manifest themselves? Are there actions that we feel content to call unquestionably the business of bankers? The starting position seems to be that of an intermediary. It is from the money-changer's bench than the word 'bank' derives, of the sort dramatically overthrown by Jesus of Nazareth. Note he did so in the Temple and it is likely that this location was chosen by these proto-bankers for the sake of security (although evidently sporadic acts of vandalism were not out of the question). They would also have wished to be beside centres of trade and commercial life and moreover the religious authorities are likely to have had either a partial or full controlling interest in their affairs. We can presume that the money-changers were predominantly acting as brokers as they conducted their business largely in public surroundings. To have held substantial deposits would have required a secure repository, such as a vault and we can assume that they would not have carried great quantities of cash about their person. The upturned tables in the Temple would have been bearing Greek, Roman, Tyrian and Jewish coinage and the money-changers would have profited presumably from a bid-offer spread made on the price of each currency in terms of the others or perhaps by way of a commission-based fee for services rendered. This business model is in every way identical to that of a modern *bureau de change* counter.

As enterprises grew and trade extended over ever greater distances, it is likely that companies would have established local offices in harbour towns and cities abroad. The money-changers would have therefore done likewise. Furthermore once trade by barter was replaced by a system of coinage (the precise date of which is disputed, but probably occurred some time early in the first millennium B.C.) an imbalance of payments would have arisen. That is to say that issues relating to cash flow would have emerged; a mechanism was needed to help enterprises safely store cash that was inert but ear-marked for future payments. It would seem that money-changers, who were already involved in the business of facilitating currency conversion, extended their service provision to allow depositing. In this way, money-changing led quite naturally to payment processing and the hosting of depository facilities. Doubtless the money-changer, if this title is still apposite, now garnered expertise and insight into many aspects of financial management. He would have been required to comprehensively understand his customers' business models, if for no other reason than to protect his own interest. And the experience he accrued we can assume was a highly marketable asset in itself; the money-changer would certainly have been sought out by prospective entrepreneurs. These were the seeds of investment banking and commercial client services. By this point, the term money-changer is a rather poor reflection of the financier's true identity. He not only exchanges coinage but takes deposits, clears payments and probably offers advice. And we can go further even than this; for with these said facilities in place (expertise, a stock of deposits, commercial relationships) the financier is ideally placed to enter or create a market for credit. Finding himself holding a quantity of coinage from a variety of customers, who in the normal course of business are highly unlikely to *simultaneously* require the return of their funds, the money-changer can become money-lender. He could lend against his deposit base and also against his own personal capital base, accrued perhaps from the profits of his other activities, and in time from those due to lending at interest. And if an application for credit is not to his liking, he might yet profit by acting as intermediary between those requiring funds for a prospect and those with excess capital to lend (the beginnings of corporate finance). Presuming depositors do not all demand the return of their funds at once, a business case can be made for lending *more* than the financier has on deposit; this is fractional reserve banking and is only a small leap of imagination away.

This story is a hypothetical account of how banking might have developed, quite naturally and organically. Some of these functions depend on the pre-existence of others, which helps with ordinal sequencing, but it is possible to conduct some of these activities in strict isolation; few are jointly co-dependent or fully mutually necessary.

Processing cash, creating physical cash (minting coin or issuing bills of exchange), advising clients, lending at interest, arranging finance by matchmaking borrowers and lenders, and direct proprietary investment from the bank's capital reserve. This list is not exhaustive by any means, but each function is certainly one which entities thought to be banks might typically perform.

Having hopefully illuminated the employment or behaviour of banks and bankers and possibly some of the social and economic triggers for their evolving such faculties, our task now is to try to unpick the knots and return to our original problem. What is the essence of banking such as makes a bank, a bank? Can we segregate the functions unequivocally so that we can provide a formal analysis of banking? Recall that a true philosophical analysis is one that provides us with a set of necessary and sufficient conditions that fully characterise a subject. It allows for testing a potential candidate's case for inclusion in the set of all instances of the subject matter. Having five daughters is sufficient to make someone a parent. Having but one child is the necessary condition. Can we reveal the necessary and sufficient (historic) functions of financiers to adequately define the concept of a bank?

In practise we certainly appear to think that one can do so. We legislate accordingly. When crises occur in the 'banking' sector we tend to blame either the banks themselves and/or the contemporary legislation, then make some sort of amendment to the rules and hope for the best. But it is my strong suspicion that the requisite analysis that would truly enable us to fully expound the *nature* of banks is unattainable, and that our attempts to do so (which are an implicit component of legislation pertaining to banking) are at best approximate and at worst fully misguided. In other words, we regulate from a presumption that the fundamental essence of banking is understood, when it patently is not. It is this that belies serial and repeated occurrence of this crisis-failure-blame-re-legislate cycle. Henry Kaufman describes[21] no less than fifteen separate crises since 1965 involving financial markets or credit markets and banking entities are implicated in every case. The legislative road has been no less bumpy in that time, with a prevailing tendency to repeal rather than enact laws, trusting ever freer markets to self-rectify. The sums involved have grown larger by turn and the consequences more serious. Any extrapolation of this trend is surely most disquieting. This matter really is of great importance.

Yet it is not unfeasible that the process of financial market regulation, which presumes that banks are identifiable as such, rests on flawed thinking. And the problem arises from the very great difficulty, or even impossibility, of analysing or defining banking in a formal way. To see why, it might be helpful to consider an analogy from an area of metaphysics that has concerned philosophers for centuries and is largely an attempt to answer the question of what makes a human being, a person. Recall from earlier the practical importance of this problem with respect to assisted suicide, abortion, the detention of suspected terrorists etc.

When asked what makes someone a person rather than merely a human being, most people will start to provide characteristics or properties that they feel are important or essential to personhood. Theoretical philosophy had attempted much the same, but in a formal setting that sought necessary and sufficient characteristics to allow testing of a proposition that 'X is a person'. And of the various suggestions, the seemingly most promising had centred on notions of autonomy, free will and self-awareness. So any human (presuming that all persons are human) who exhibited autonomy and exercised their will in a self-aware fashion might be considered 'a person'. We can then test this analysis against our ordinary conception to see how it measures up. An infant for example may not in fact be considered a full person since they are not sufficiently cognitively developed to be autonomous. Or the brain trauma victim in a so-called persistently vegetative state might also be deemed a non-person owing to their lack of self-awareness or an ability to exercise their will. However promising this analysis seems to be, it runs into difficulties. Aside from being rather difficult to separate cleanly, the set of conditions run into one of the most ancient theoretical brick walls in philosophy, namely the problem of free will in a deterministic world. Put briefly, if the world is deterministic i.e. fully predictable for all eternity and if the current state of affairs is fully known, then in what sense is our will free? Every action we take, we were always going to take, as anyone who happened to know the complete state of the world beforehand could have foreseen. And if we cannot avoid these preset outcomes, how can we be considered to have autonomy? The problem of free will under determinism has a vast literature and its impact on classical theories of personhood has generally been to create an *impasse*.

But in 1962, a novel approach was suggested by philosopher Peter Strawson.[22] He proposed a way out of the conundrum by supposing that an analysis of the standard, formal kind that had previously been sought was implausible. Instead we should consider personhood to be a property that emerges from social relations. This shifts the emphasis away from attempts to define a person as someone who exhibits properties a, b and c or who has function x, y or z, and re-configures our perspective to see personhood as a concept that simply emerges or evolves of its own accord from a society of people relating to one another. Given this, our attempt at defining by demanding a set criterion or checklist of features a person must have, is methodologically flawed. It may *approximate* the theoretical notion of personhood, perhaps even reasonably well, but it might be akin to attempting to define a boat without reference to water. In short, we cannot extract its essence or true nature from the circumstance in which it occurs or has meaning.

This is not a simple idea to appreciate, but its applicability to the analysis of banking is perhaps clearer than that of the conceptually more abstract notion of personhood. My contention is that banking is not reducible, and nor can it be extricated, from the complex commercial environment from which is emerges. Banking, and indeed all financial activity, is not simply straightforwardly analogous or even comparable to other business activity. We may understand say automobile manufacturers with only an elementary definition and without recourse to other segments of the economy and social system for clarity. But banking cannot reasonably be understood in this manner. 'Auto manufacturer' is an analytical phrase; its meaning can be unpicked by simple comprehension of the words. But 'bank' is not analytically recoverable. And when we attempt to pin down the meaning of banking with precision, the results are ill-fitting and misshapen.

Now consider the implications of this hypothesis if true. How often have plaintive cries been made by politician since the crisis of 2008 for banks to return to doing what they are 'supposed' to do, which is presumed to be providing basic clearing functions and lending prudently to business. Yet this call for a return to a pure and simple form of banking is wholly misguided if banking is considered, as I suggest, as being an emergent property of a complex economy. Since banking under this reading is inseparable from its hosting system, such calls are tantamount to desiring the entire financial and economic system to be re-wound. To revert to a time when all banks did was clear payments, swap currency and issue commercial loans is impossible without re-setting much of modern life, *even though we may not be certain precisely how banks have contributed to this complexity*. And besides this, even if banks were restricted to functions supposedly at the core of their essence as of yesteryear, one might struggle to pinpoint when the 'golden age' occurred. For example, although Adam Smith in the *Wealth of Nations* understands the benefits of credit to trade, he places strict limits on precisely the sort of lending by banks to companies for fixed capital investment purposes that the current generation of politicians seem to believe should be banks' *raison d'etre*. He writes;

"The returns of the fixed capital are in almost all cases much slower than those of the circulating capital; and such expenses, even when laid out with the greatest prudence and judgement, very seldom return to the undertaker till after a period of many years, a period by far too distant to suit the conveniency of a bank" [23]

Extraordinary. Smith, to many the father of sensible and seemly free market capitalism, is indicating that the banks should not look at long term capital-intensive projects of the precise sort today's politicians and economic advisors would have us believe banks have a duty to facilitate. Instead, he seems to suggest banks deploy their capital in short dated opportunities. Whether he meant of the sort vilified of late, of extremely limited horizons, is debatable. But his advising *against* banks involving themselves in long term capital projects is unambiguous.

The overarching point here is not however to argue for what banks should or should not do, but to indicate the futility of calling for a return to some erstwhile idealised form of banking. Not only is the history of banking for all time, one of serial crises and collapses, it is *necessarily* so, since it merely reflects, as it must, the nature and happenings of the society from which it emerges. As developed economies have progressed to levels of complexity at ever increasing rates of change, emergent banking practices have both fed off and in turn fuelled this erratic motion. It cannot logically be otherwise, in my estimation, by virtue of the ontological nature of banking. And though we attempt to regulate and understand banks in isolation, their inherent inseparability from society renders such method approximate at best or fatally flawed at worst. This may seem like a counsel of despair; that any attempt at manipulating the system for the better is intrinsically doomed to fail. But it is not meant to be taken in this spirit. The real aim of these proposals is to dispel the idea that understanding and regulating banks is a simple matter. Much more thought needs to be given as to what they are and why crises involving them occur so readily and to that end, a rather different perspective to the current orthodoxy ought to be considered.

5.

"The point of philosophy is to start with something so simple as not to seem worth stating, and to end with something so paradoxical that no-one will believe it".

Bertrand Russell, *The Philosophy of Logical Atomism*

Banks, derivatives and value, we might think of as entities, instruments and a concept respectively, although to do so at the commencement of an investigation into their true nature is formally question-begging. This is a common trap, to be avoided. If we ask what is the essence of the entity we call a bank, we have already made presumption in the question as to the format of the answer, for we have already assumed a bank to be an entity. As has been suggested, a bank may just be a collective of bankers whose activities are very hard to isolate from the wider economic and social structure in which they operate. Likewise for the 'concept' of value; assuming value is conceptual from the outset, also begs the question being posed.

By picking what are generally considered an entity, an instrument and a concept and subjecting them to philosophical scrutiny, it should be apparent that it is far from straightforward to perfectly characterize or define with complete confidence. And yet subject matter just such as these are commonly considered perfectly well understood. When commentators talk of banks acting as they ought to, they do not seem to mean this in the philosophical sense that particular banks should aim to reflect the essential nature of the ideal bank. What is really meant is that banks should perform certain specific functions and avoid others. There are two very different stances. In the light of the recent debacle and given the on-going recurrence of such events, it is no longer sufficient to merely suggest that practices need better regulating or that instruments should have restrictions of one sort or another placed on their use. It is imperative first to understand *why* these financial entities seem so apt to lurch from one disaster to the next. And this work should no longer proceed with untested assumptions in place. We must cease to presume that we know what exists in financial markets and that we comprehend the true nature of all the entities, instruments and concepts of which they are constituted. Until such time, we will continue not only in wilful ignorance but with little insight as to the extent of our ignorance. In no other field of human existence are we so acutely deficient and, worse, indifferent to our being so. From matters as disparate as political science and medical ethics to educational theory and social psychology, we have advanced by due consideration of what exists, without prejudice, and acknowledging the limits of our comprehension.

Although formally this is metaphysical work, the labelling is inessential. It is a spirit of enquiry and a method of analysis hitherto unused in the study of the financial markets. When one questions elemental ideas that have become ingrained, when one asks what is an A, or what makes a B a B, as the quotation from Russell suggests, the path can lead from misplaced surety to considered confusion. Whilst neither is optimal, much can be learned from the journey between the former and the latter, and this is often the true merit of sustained, dogged enquiry. If we wish to know why something is as it is, it is almost always profitable to consider *what* that something is in the first instance. If we wish to know why banks acted as recklessly as we think they did, why they seemed content *en masse* to take risks that threatened their very existence (and which basic business economics suggests should not be the case) or why derivatives have proliferated exponentially and can now wreck giant multinational companies in days, or again if we wish to know how real estate prices bubbled and collapsed whilst associated bundles of mortgages came to be so mis-marked that banks had to write down their value time and time again, we must begin with first principles. The philosophy of language has enjoyed a star role in philosophical circles from the early 20th century onwards, whereby theories due to Wittgenstein and others suggested that the nature of philosophical truths, meaning and problems, may all be bound up in the language which is necessarily used in their investigation. Some felt this rendered the problems, such as whether God exists or whether there are objective moral standards, as mere semantic riddles that occur simply as a consequence of language itself. But regardless of whether such ideas are correct, the importance of language as a contextual backdrop to every thoughtful enquiry should not be forgotten. Put simply, we should not presume to understand the terms used in relation to financial markets or any other walks of life, without due consideration. And it is fully conceivable that an exposition of the true nature of what *exists* in the financial markets, will lead to clarity as to *why* things are the way they are and whether they can indeed be made to be different.

Chapter 4

1.

Derivatives are explosive. One dollar invested in an option contract that has a one month lifespan may disappear completely (i.e. a 100% loss in a month) or be worth 50 dollars (a 5000% return) or more. Almost nothing is out of the question in this regard. Managing such violent, exponential and dangerous activity is more akin to rocket science than banking. And in this light, the banks did the sensible thing; they hired rocket scientists.

Sadly however, the analogy is imperfect. Derivatives may have been called financial weapons of mass destruction by Warren Buffett, but their chaotic, stochastic flight-paths have little in common with the Newtonian predictability of a tube pointing up with its thrusting engine pointing down. Worse still, as they slipped out of the white coats and into Saville Row suits, the men of science left behind in their laboratories the philosophical theories that belied their practical expertise.

The philosophy of science considers the nature of scientific work. What is science? How should scientific knowledge be gleaned? What is a theory? And so on and so forth. Given that the earliest philosophers have claim to also being the earliest scientists, it is perhaps unsurprising that the birth of the philosophy of science was largely synchronous with the birth of science itself. As Aristotle began a rudimentary, but nevertheless ambitious, taxonomy of the natural world in earnest, it is impossible to imagine that he set this aside from his work on metaphysics, logic and epistemology. The parallel between any underlying theory or Law of Nature (even in a simple form of folk law or natural aphorism) and Plato's metaphysical notions of Universals[24] must surely have been apparent to the Greeks.

If Universals were the thoughts of the Gods and the Gods created the world, theorizing in any general way would be an attempt to see the world through the eyes of the Gods. This would be one way to describe the philosophy of science.

Even in the fraction of Aristotle's known works that have survived, there are very few stones of life left unturned. Justice, logic, Pythagoreanism, animals, poetry, rhetoric, pleasure and astronomy are but a selection of the fields into which he made enquiry and about which he wrote extensively. That so many of Aristotle's conclusions have been fully debunked and in many cases led humanity to wander down blind alleys for some two millennia is rather beside the point; there are surprisingly few scientific theories that are indubitably true and not subject to revision in time. Possibly the greatest of all polymaths, Aristotle sought truth wherever he looked. Everything he did was philosophical first and foremost. He catalogued assiduously, using largely descriptive methods with little in the way of data or experiment. To modern eyes and in the light of professional science, the work has the feel of an extremely zealous amateur, but of course context is everything. That a competent A Level mathematics student knows more of calculus than Leibniz ever did is not remarkable: it is the vision to conceive such theory before others that is the hallmark of original scholarship.

So astounding was Aristotle's output that his pronouncements on many subjects were seen as beyond reproach until the birth of modern science in the 17th Century. The stranglehold on thought kept by the Western Christian church encompassed Aristotelian and Platonic ideas (following the work of early and late medieval thinkers to harmonise these classical philosophies and Christian doctrine), with predictable consequences for the Renaissance humanist who tried to think beyond Hellenistic thought, if not necessarily beyond Christian orthodoxy. But as science and progress took hold, questioning Aristotelian natural philosophy led seamlessly to an evaluation of science itself. The philosophy of science began to be given more formal consideration.

As always, the application of philosophical techniques to a specific area of interest will involve a blend of metaphysics, logic, epistemology, ethics and so forth. In the case of the philosophy of science, we might ask what is science or what can we know by scientific means? Is there any such thing as good science or morally just science? Is there even beautiful or ugly science? Asking, and attempting to answer, such questions, provides scientists and philosophers of science with a very helpful framework in which to work. By questioning the feasibility of their undertaking and seeking to understand the limitations of what might be learned, scientific procedure is instilled with an added rigour and robustness.

Now consider transporting a scientist from a laboratory to a trading desk and expecting him to "do science" in the financial markets. What might this mean? Well evidently the hope is that the scientist will be able to apply the techniques (especially the highly quantitative ones) they have been trained to use for scientific purposes, profitably in the financial markets. Note the two critical, implicit assumptions here; firstly that scientific techniques are appropriate in a financial situation and secondly that the philosophical ideas that have supported the development of these scientific techniques are also transferable.

So how should one gauge the validity of these assumptions? A convenient method is to simply consider some of the problems that philosophers of science have pondered and to see what impact this might have on the work of a financial scientist (or a "quant" as they are often known). Using the term financial scientist may be to commit the fallacy of begging the question since the outcome of our investigation into the assumptions might be that no such person can exist. Firstly however, it is worth briefly discussing the types of trading activity in the markets for which purpose scientists are employed. The basis for a speculative trade made by a bank, hedge fund or proprietary trading group, can be fundamental, quantitative, arbitrage, intuition or simple herd-following (or its counter-part, contrarianism) and more else besides. Let us consider each in turn.

A fundamental trade will have as its justification some notion that the underlying situation in a company or economy, a market or an instrument, is incorrectly reflected by the price of the security. So, for example, an analyst may study a company and conclude that given its revenue, prospects, levels of debt and assets, its management structure and the state of its competitors and the economy as a whole, that it is likely to be more profitable than the market as a whole expects and may therefore pay a higher dividend in consequence than is currently forecast. Typically in a bank, the analyst himself is likely to be paid to produce research along these lines and is not then expected to trade on the conclusion. The research is more likely to be used by the bank as marketing material to be sent to clients who may then decide to follow the advice. An asset manager on the other hand may conduct such research himself or simply collate research notes written by various banks and form his own judgement. Either way, fundamental trading is not commonly attended to by quants, unless a quantitative model has some supposed fundamental underpinnings.

Herd-following, also known as piggy-backing, may or may not have a quantitative side to it. Some traders will simply leap on to a bandwagon that is reported in the financial press or on the news wires. It is not uncommon to hear a trader when questioned as to why he is buying a stock, replying "Because it is going up". There is an obvious ambiguity to this statement which is probably intentional and is, in short, an admission that the justification is flimsy. It is not clear whether the trader means he has now bought because it has gone up recently or if he means it in a more predictive manner i.e. it is going to go up. Thus it tells one little that could not be presumed; would a trader be buying if he thought the stock was going down? Others still, will be buying because they have heard others are. The essence of such trades is momentum; the trader believes the price of the security has momentum in one direction and he is picking up on the trend and hoping that the price will travel further on its current course, rendering him profitable. There is an entire sub-industry in the financial markets dedicated to the discovery of such trends which ranges in sophistication from trading purely on the strength of market gossip to highly developed statistical modelling. For now, let us just consider that quants will often be involved in this field. The near-opposite method of trading, which is contrarianism, has much in common with momentum trading. The aim here is to spot an asset which has indeed trended in one direction but is due for a sharp reversal. The momentum trader sees an asset flying higher and perceives an opportunity to buy, expecting even greater moves northward. The contrarian sees the same price action but draws the opposite conclusion and sells. A related term here is mean-reversion, which refers to the notion that the price of a security may have some meaningful average price to which it might be expected to return after significant moves away. There is a tension between momentum trading (with its maxim 'The trend is your friend') and contrarian or mean-reversion strategies.

Arbitrage is a term used inaccurately to describe a great deal of trading. In its strictest and most formal sense, to arbitrage a security (known as 'to arb' in the market) is to take advantage of its trading at two different locations, at two different prices. Some securities are listed (i.e. they trade) in multiple locations and other things being equal they should always trade at the same price. If the security is fungible, that is to say fully transferable at no cost between the two locations, then any discrepancy in the price of the security in the two locations represents an opportunity for profit. Simply buy the cheaper version, sell the dearer and have your back office transfer the long and short position and pocket the difference in the purchase and sale price. Now before the markets traded electronically, arbitrage opportunities could be present unbeknownst to traders since their existence was a function of the impossibility of someone knowing the price of a security in two places at once. This could even be true in a *single* stock exchange; when stocks traded in a pit-based environment it was possible, especially in a chaotic market, for a stock to trade at two different prices in the same pit, albeit temporarily. As the markets became electronic, there was a brief window when some instruments traded in open-outcry pits and 'on the screens' simultaneously and arbitrage was again possible; this involved a trader 'upstairs' executing trades via the electronic order book and telephoning a colleague in a pit to complete the arbitrage. The risk was that they would be too slow in completing the 'arb' and would consequently be 'hung' on 'one leg'. A great deal of terminology to describe something so simple! In trying to execute an arbitrage, the traders must buy the instrument in one place and sell in another. If they buy in one place and then attempt to sell in another but miss the best price (the 'bid' price) and the instrument starts to fall in value, then they are exposed since they simply own the instrument outright. This is the risk of the arbitrage trade and is known as the risk of being 'hung'. Approximately, the trade is worthwhile if the number of winners multplied by the profit from each trade exceeds the number of times the arbitrageurs will be hung multplied by the loss from each hanging. Even after the markets became overwhelmingly electronic, arbitrage continued to exist until software was written to execute the arbitrage in both (or more) markets automatically. At this point, an arms race developed whereby the speed of execution was the key to success. In the early 1990s, an electronic arbitrage might be successful if it could achieve speeds measured in tenths of a second. By 2000, the necessary speed was generally under a few hundred milliseconds and in 2010 is under a few hundred microseconds. The race for speed saw firms hiring office space within yards of the various Exchanges' telecommunication hubs to gain an edge. Computers of the highest specification were, and are, used. This never-ending battle for silicon supremacy comes at high cost, and arbitrage is no longer a mainstream activity for many banks or trading firms, but is left to high-tech, high-frequency, low latency specialists. Arbitrage has interesting philosophical properties which will be discussed in due course, particularly in relation to logical deduction. The essential simplicity of a pure arbitrage has not generally warranted the attention of a quant; super-computers, not super-brains, are the order of the day. The aforementioned misappropriation of the term arbitrage by certain quantitative traders also has many interesting philosophical implications, as we shall see.

There are traders whose strategic motive is little more than intuition. 'Feeling the force'. Easily mocked, (particularly by quants and also by academic finance theorists), there are undoubtedly successful traders who seem to do little other than gauge the sentiment in the market by a feeling in their bones and hence derive a sentiment for the likely direction of prices. Routinely this is explained away by behavioural social scientists as an example of survivor bias; take half a dozen traders who are trading on their wits alone and you will find half are profitable, half loss making, one of the six will be very successful and one very unsuccessful (compare with six traders rolling a die with the number of spots representing their success). The resultant 'profit and loss' profile of the traders/monkeys in a lab, will lead us to think one monkey is a great trader, one abysmal, one is good, one is bad and two are pretty average. I find this argument both persuasive yet inadequate; indeed the theory is almost an example of survivor bias itself. However, in my experience, the theory is unable to account for the trader who trades intuitively for years on end with great success. I have been told by academics that this is simply a long run of good luck; that if we took 10,000 traders, some would by dint of pure chance trade profitably for years. This is like a version of one of the most celebrated broker scams which involves messaging 10,000 potential clients, half with a forecast that a stock will rise, half with the forecast that it will fall. The following day, the 5,000 clients who received the correct forecast are contacted again, 2,500 with a forecast for the stock to rise, 2,500 with a forecast for a decline. This is repeated until a handful of clients believe the broker has direct contact with Hermes, God of Trading himself, and it is at this point that the broker demands a fee for further forecasts or takes their order to trade and collects a commission. Survivor bias theory suggests that the handful of traders receiving the final free message from the artful broker are no different to the traders who have traded profitably for years (or days) successfully. What this omits however is the personalities involved and the cut-throat market in which they operate. I shall not offer a theory here as to why I believe some traders can use intuition successfully. Any claim would probably rely on intuition itself given the unlikelihood of traders subjecting themselves to a controlled test. There is an old joke concerning traders of the flashy, ostentatious variety whose quantitative skills were decidedly not the secret of their success; that it has a truthful ring is perhaps circumstantial evidence that intuitive trading is not plain gambling.[25] In short, I have seen enough traders use intuition and fall by the wayside to agree with the theorists, but those few who have had long term success in this way always have something else about them; wit, recklessness, courage, sharpness or some such quality. Never have I encountered a failed trader with even one of these qualities in sufficient measure.

Trading in this way either has negligible scientific grounding or a very deep understanding of the human psyche which is well beyond current cognitive and psychological knowledge. And good fortune is a necessary condition for long term trading success, but not a sufficient condition. The philosophical aspects to intuitive trading are more epistemic than scientific, raising questions surrounding what knowledge such traders have and how they obtain this knowledge. Questions of perception arise.

Of the other trading methodologies, quantitative trading is perhaps the most pertinent to matters relating to the philosophy of science. Quantitative strategies involve the application of mathematical and statistical techniques to arrive at trading decisions. The human input once the model is running will vary. A model that runs without any intervention, after having been switched on, is known as pure "black box". There is a great deal of ground between traders using some but only minimal quantitative techniques and those running black box systems. But overall, systematic or programme trading (as it is also known) now accounts for vast amounts of the exchange traded volume in securities, and perhaps even the majority. Quantitative trading need not take place on an exchange. A common set-up for a bank desk would be to have a team of quants pricing securities via sophisticated models, a team of traders using the output from these models to offer up prices to 'sales traders' who then tout the prices to clients to try to win trades. This basic business model is found across the industry from teams trading equity derivatives to credit default swap divisions and CDO operations. If the team trade 'on the telly' (i.e. on an electronic exchange) there will also be a computer scientist on the desk or one of the team (almost invariably a quant) will have strong programming skills. Quantitative trading is carried out by investment banks, hedge funds, proprietary trading firms and, in a limited form, by day-traders in their bedrooms. They all have 'a system' which involves numerical inputs and signal outputs. The input is usually data; price data, volume data, open interest figures, economic data etc. The output signal is usually buy, sell or do nothing. This is of course a simplification of such systems.

An important and popular form of quantitative trading is statistical arbitrage or stat-arb. Like much quantitative trading, this relies heavily on statistical and mathematical models to trade securities that are thought to be strongly related. The holding period for groups of securities (typically, long some and short others) might be a matter of seconds. The technology involved in this trading is considerable; high specification machines capable of making calculations across potentially thousands of assets. The trade will be executed automatically within a few hundred microseconds and the risk of the position will be monitored in real time. An example of a stat-arb strategy might be one that watches a dozen commodity futures and prices them relatively to one another. If a large order appears in one market, temporarily displacing it, the stat-arb system will explode into life, attempting to trade against the large order and hedging the risk by trading a basket of the other commodities in the opposite direction. This will take fractions of a second. If the model and the strategy are effective, the risk of the portfolio that this trade creates should be very low and the black box machine will now monitor the situation to attempt to reverse out of the trade at some point. A simple stat-arb then might see a large buyer of gold futures, attempt to sell some as the price is temporarily forced higher by the buyer, and hedge the exposure by buying a selection of other precious metals (silver, palladium etc). This leaves what is known as a spread position; long something, short something else. Now for related securities, this should be a lower risk position than just an outright position in one or other of the securities; if the machine buys gold and does not hedge the position it is exposed to all the fluctuations in the price of gold. However if it has hedged by selling some silver, then a fall in the price of gold might be offset by a corresponding fall in the price of silver, thus recouping some, or all, or even more than the losses on the gold position. This elementary idea belies most stat-arb trades although the complexity that can be embedded is, for practical purposes, almost limitless.

This broad brush discussion of the types of proprietary trading that occur is not exhaustive. It has said little of the approach taken by longer term investors such as asset managers, pension funds and insurance funds. However the use of quants and of scientists generally in the financial markets is most prominent in the areas of short term speculation, complex derivatives and high frequency, low latency automated trading. As noted, this accounts for a vast amount of the daily turnover both on and off exchanges around the world.

2.

Both traders and philosophers enjoy a good argument, although they are usually talking about different things. A good argument between traders is likely to be aggressive, brief and end with money changing hands. Between philosophers, it may last for several hundred years and will usually end up with someone or everyone denying the existence of something or everything. When quants or traders create a new strategy they are in effect making an argument. They will have a number of reasons why a trade has the potential to be profitable. The reasons will suggest a conclusion that is in effect a trading decision. This bears comparison to an extent with a formal philosophical argument. In philosophy, and especially modern analytic philosophy, an argument typically takes the form of a number of premises and a conclusion. These premises will be assertions about some state of affairs (according to the argument) and they should lead, by logical reasoning, to the argument's conclusion. Now there is a most fundamental distinction to be drawn at this point, the importance of which it is hard to overstate. This is the distinction between an argument that is deductive and one that is inductive.

A deductive argument is one whose conclusion follows logically from the premises. For example,

> Premise: All bankers are clever.
> Premise: John is a banker.
> Conclusion: John is clever.

This argument is deductive. The premises entail the conclusion since, given 1. and 2., 3. *must* be true, as it is simply embedded in the premises. Aristotle is given particular credit for this form of argument (but to our best knowledge, he did not make this specific argument concerning bankers) known as a syllogism. The essential point to note is that if the premises are true, then the conclusion must logically also be true; philosophers refer to this property as *validity*. This syllogism is formally valid; it is not possible for the premises to be true and the conclusion false. Furthermore, the argument is described as *sound* if the argument is formally valid *and* the premises are indeed true (one suspects premise 1. may raise eyebrows). One might therefore contest whether this argument is sound even though it does appear formally valid. An argument is additionally described as persuasive or *cogent* if it is convincing *and* sound. Therefore an argument that is philosophically cogent is sound and if it is sound it is valid, by definition. A cogent argument is the strongest argument of all.

Arguments are often presented masquerading as formally deductive because the truly cogent, deductive argument is a rare and very powerful thing indeed. In reality, almost all of our reasoning is conducted in an *inductive* fashion. Induction is the process of arguing from a limited set of observations to a broad generalisation. For example,

Premise: Every banker Smith knows is stupid.
Conclusion: All bankers are stupid.

The difference between this argument and the deductive argument should be fairly stark. The premise does not lead logically to the conclusion. The argument simply does not feel as watertight. It seems to provoke further questions such as how many bankers has Smith met? How many would be necessary to justify the conclusion? Even if Smith knows every banker in the world except one, the conclusion is still not fully entailed by the premise.

Inductive reasoning constitutes the overwhelming majority of our everyday opinion-forming habits. Since the truly deductive argument is so hard to come by, to avoid dithering in perpetuity, we rely on induction to make general judgements about the state of the world. We may not consider the problem in such dry theoretical terms as these but this is how, viewed formally, we live in practice; we move from a limited set of information to the creation of generalisations.

For philosophers of science, the problem of induction looms very large indeed. If one accepts the aim of science is to uncover truths about the world, to reveal the workings and laws of nature (and all of this is contentious, but bear with it), then the problem of induction is only too real, since no matter how many experiments one conducts, and regardless of how clearly the data points in one direction, any generalisation formed via inductive argument is not logically foolproof. Intelligence testing of 99.999% of the world's bankers does not allow one to say with all certainty that the intelligence of all bankers is sub-normal.

An obvious response is that this is all rather pedantic; when the evidence all points the same way, surely there comes a time when one is happy to accept the conclusion as proven? The problem of induction though has not been solved by this process, merely side-stepped. The evidence may be convincing, but it only takes one clever banker to disprove the argument's conclusion (by his existence, not by his cunning rhetoric).

How does this relate to the financial markets? Consider again the arbitrage strategy. This involved the buying and selling of an identical security in different locations at profitable prices. The 'argument' for this trade has a deductive element to it. [26]

1. Premise: Price p_1 can be paid for security X
2. Premise: Security X can be sold at price p_2
3. Premise: $p_1 < p_2$
4. Conclusion: X can be traded profitably and without risk.

This argument is very strong. It appears valid since 1.,2. and 3. certainly indicate 4. must be true; recall that to be formally sound the argument must be valid and the premises must be true. Premises 1.-3. seem to be statements that we might be reasonably comfortable accepting. Ignoring philosophical issues regarding the nature of knowledge, what we can know with certainty etc., it does seem likely that traders would indeed know at what price they can trade a security at any given time (premises 1. and 2.) and premise 3. should be trivially calculable. Therefore one could make the case that the truth of all the premises is knowable in reality. We cannot say in this instance if the premises are true but in particular cases this should be ascertainable. Finally then, is the argument persuasive? Well does risk-free profit sound appealing?

An arbitrage is an enormously mouth-watering prospect for traders. Formally delineating the argument shows it to have a highly deductive structure and as has been noted, the truly deductive argument is a rarity. The validity of the argument means that the conclusion is guaranteed to be true if the premises are true and the conclusion of this argument is the Holy Grail for any trading strategy.

For the arbitrage to deliver, one has to probe the premises further for weaknesses. This becomes a question of logistics rather than logic as premises 1.-3. need to be true *contemporaneously* and for the specific firm in question. The trading firm may agree that 1.-3. are true if and only if one has an extremely competitive method of executing trades electronically. So product X may be offered (i.e. for sale) at p_1 but do they have a fast enough technical connection to the exchange to be able to pay p_1 before others do? These issues however are entirely separate from the underlying strategy; if the firm believes the premises to be true and that it has the capability to act on them, then it will make risk-free profits.

Sadly, however, arbitrage opportunities are not so easily found. For securities that trade on multiple exchanges, the price discrepancy will be kept minimal by incredibly fast black-box (automated) systems. The move to electronic order books has of course meant that a security on one exchange has but one price at any given moment. Nevertheless the allure of arbitrage is too great for traders to give up so easily.

Consider the following different trading strategy written as a formal argument.

1. Premise: Price p1 can be paid for security X
2. Premise: Security Y can be sold at price p2
3. Premise: Securities X and Y are almost identical.
4. Premise: $p1 < p2$
5. Conclusion: X and Y can be traded profitably and without risk.

This is an inductive argument hiding behind a mask of deduction. Premise 3 is critical to this argument's success. In the case of the arbitrage when X and Y were identical ie $X \equiv Y$, the argument had a generalizing power that is now absent. In what sense are X and Y *almost* identical? Are they almost identical all of the time? X cannot cease to be X, but could X and Y cease to be very similar?

One solution to this bug is to weaken the conclusion.

5.*Conclusion: X and Y can be traded profitably and with low risk.

Now although this gives the argument preferable formal grounds, it has done so at considerable expense. The gap between low risk and zero risk (infinite from a certain mathematical viewpoint) stems from the gap introduced between security X and Y not being simply X. But the concession made in the conclusion does little to stop the doubts that are creeping in. What is low risk? Is it simply related to the similarity of X and Y, in which case, has the concession bought the argument any extra credibility?

The essence of the problem is that arbitrage has a deductive quality that is wildly appealing to traders, but that a strategy which is not a strict arbitrage ceases to be deductive. The line of division between deduction and induction is fully distinct but many traders and quants forget or wilfully overlook this. If they propose a strategy that uses instrument Y as a close proxy for X, they have made an inductive assertion that having observed Y they believe it to be very similar to X.

One subtle and partial exception to this is in the use of derivatives. Given standard definitions of futures, options, swaps and swaptions it is possible to synthetically re-create any of these products using a selection of the others. A common example explained in many introductory derivatives texts is that a futures contract can be synthetically manufactured using a call and a put option of duration equal to one another. Briefly, define a call option as the right but not the obligation to pay 100 dollars (the strike price) for a futures contract. The corresponding put gives the owner the right but not the obligation to sell the future at a price of 100 dollars. Suppose the future is trading at 101 dollars, then the call option must be worth at least 1 dollar (since it gives the owner the right to buy the futures for 100 dollars). The call is described as in-the-money, since its strike price is below where the future is currently trading. The put is out-of-the-money since its strike price is also below where the future is trading and it gives the right to sell not buy. However, the put may not be worthless and the call may be worth more than just 1 dollar. This is because, assuming the options have some time left before expiry, they will still have some *time value*. Time value reflects the possibility that the options may yet become in-the-money in the case of the put or further in-the-money in the case of the call, before they expire. Although the put is *intrinsically* worthless with the future trading above its strike price, it will have some *extrinsic* value if there is sufficient time before it expires and if the underlying contract into which it may be converted is expected to be sufficiently volatile. So if the put option has a month of life remaining and the future typically moves 1 dollar per day in either direction, then the put option has a considerable chance of expiring in-the-money and this will be reflected in its current price.

Consider this example of a synthetic arbitrage using futures and options. The 100 dollar call is trading at 0.16, the 100 dollar put is trading at 1.52 dollars and the future into which the options expire is trading at 98.50 dollars. Buying the future, selling the call and buying the put is profitable *regardless of where the futures are trading* when the options expire. Below is the payoff profile to this strategy at various levels of future price at expiration.

Synthetic arbitrage strategy payoffs at expiration

	99	100	101
Short 100 Call	0.16	0.16	-0.84
Long 100 Put	-0.52	-1.52	-1.52
Long future	0.5	1.5	2.5
NET Payoff	**0.14**	**0.14**	**0.14**

With the contracts expiring at a futures price of 100, the call is worthless and has been sold at 0.16 dollars; the put, for which 1.52

dollars was paid, is worthless; whilst the long future position has made a 1.50 dollar profit. The net profit from the strategy is invariable with respect to the settlement price of the futures contract.

So if the future can be bought more cheaply than the synthetic future (the combination of the put and the call) can be sold, the payoff to this strategy (buying the future, selling the synthetic) should be fixed and risk-free. On the face of it, the outcome is no different to a simple arbitrage of the future itself. This seems to be a counter-example that shows a deductive-type strategy is possibly using non-identical contracts. However, although the contracts are non-identical in name, the combined long call/short put position is *functionally* identical to a long futures contract position and indeed will often expire into the futures contract (i.e. at expiration, the call and put literally become futures contracts if exercised) or all three contracts (futures, call and put) expire into the same underlying product or even into cash.

The counter-example is a powerful philosophical weapon. A single, valid counter-example is enough to invalidate an entire theory. The case of synthetic derivatives as an arbitrage however is not sufficient to support the notion that arbitrage can be extended to non-identical contracts without reliance on induction, since the arbitrage exists only by the contracts' defined purpose. That is, in so far as the contracts exist at all, they do so simply as a defined payoff profile. If the payoff to a contract is some function $P(.)$ then a strategy may be declared to be deductively supported if the synthetic counterpart to the contract used in the arbitrage also has payoff function $P(.)$ for all time and circumstance.

There is a vast array of strategies in operation in the world's financial markets that are known broadly as stat-arb. However, I believe "statistical arbitrage" to be a dangerous misnomer. Arbitrage in its strictest sense is limited to the buying and selling of one contract simultaneously for profit. Synthetic arbitrage is the buying and selling of a contract and its synthetically identical equivalent. Statistical arbitrage, however, is purely a form of spread trading. Spread trading is a mean-reversion strategy that relies on two or more securities having a statistical relationship that should, given past experience, revert to some sort of average price. There are many names for this style of trading; long-short, pair-wise, relative value, to name but three. Stat-arb generally refers to such spread trading but in a highly automated and extra short term fashion. A stat-arb fund may track a collection of say health care stocks and derivatives. It will have estimates of how these instruments should move together, enumerated in terms of the correlation or covariance or as perhaps a market beta or industry beta. Awaiting a temporary distortion in one of the instruments, it will pounce on the outlier and hedge with the other products.

But stat-arb is not an arbitrage. Arbitrage has an aura of irrefutability which derives from its deductive foundation. It is clear why a stat-arb fund might wish to align itself with arbitrage strategies. But the strategic method of a stat-arb is to move from a particular set of data from which the correlations between instruments are estimated to a general rule or law about how such instruments must move. This is pure induction; from limited data set to generalisation.

Why does this matter? Certainly, there are some wildly successful stat-arb funds generating vast profit for their owners. Nevertheless, stat-arb has a fallibility to it that even the name might be an attempt to disguise. To argue that "everyone knows" it is not a literal arbitrage leads one to question why it is therefore so-named. The danger of stat-arb is that by invoking the deductive persuasiveness of an arbitrage, it becomes easy to understate the risk of a trade. And this has wreaked havoc in the financial markets.

The argument put forward by stat-arb traders would run along these lines. Here are some instruments that are highly correlated. In our back-testing they never diverge by more than a% and they return to these long run averages in b% of cases within t days/hours/minutes/ seconds. Sure, this is not an arbitrage but the products are so similar that it is very similar to an arbitrage and therefore the risk is minimal.

This reasoning is dangerous. A trade is an arbitrage or it is not. If it is possible for the buy and the sell side to have payoff functions that are not precise mirror-images, then the trade is not an arbitrage. Given that, the payoff function for a non-arbitrage strategy as a whole is therefore unknowable with certainty. In philosophical terms, an argument is either deductive or it is not deductive. *Almost* deductive, is inductive.

The false sense of security that the word arbitrage lends can cause catastrophic results in two ways. The first is that when spreads start to move in a manner not commensurate with the model, the instinct is to increase the size of the position i.e. the bet. Suppose apples usually trade at a 10 pence premium to pears and that the spread (in other words, the difference) between their two prices only varies a couple of pence per day, so in the 8p to 12p range. Suddenly apples are trading at only a 5 pence premium to pears. Now this did not happen in the data set used to construct the strategy, so one starts to think that this is a huge opportunity; one buys more apples and sells short more pears. But then apples and pears trade at flat (i.e. the same price) and the strategy is showing a horrible loss. Still, this is almost an arbitrage, right? Buy more apples and sell more pears and wait for the bounce in apple price or the collapse in the pear price. Oh good grief; pears trading at a premium to apples now. Clearing house knocking at the door. Risk department have been fired. Security guards are ready to escort the stat-arb team off the desk.

The second problem is that the capital reserve set against the trade is likely to be too low. This has certainly been the case during the recent financial crisis for the overwhelming majority of inductive trades (which is most trades). The trade is purported to be low risk and in normal market conditions probably gives that appearance. Apples and pears trade roughly 10 pence apart with little variation. Any spread position that the firm has in these contracts is not likely to require a great deal of margin set against it (the clearing houses rely on similar methods to set the risk parameters as the traders use to devise the strategy). Given this, it is quite manageable for firms to run several such strategies or perhaps several *thousand*; apples versus mangoes, bananas versus grapes etc. etc. But when the market undergoes a major basis-changing event, such a portfolio of strategies is unlikely to have the diversification necessary to protect the firm. The perceived and actual risk is liable to explode from very low to catastrophic. Firms can blow out not just on the size of their losses but on the requirement to make large cash deposits to cover the margin of their positions.

Much has been made lately of the so-called "Black Swan" phenomenon, whereby the theory that all swans were white (an inductive assertion which seemed reasonable given the dataset at the time consistent entirely of white swans), was invalidated by the counter-example of a single black swan. So with stat-arb, seemingly reasonable trading ideas are subject to the emergence of conditions that diverge extraordinarily with the previous experience from which the ideas were born. This cannot happen to a genuine arbitrage strategy. And the explanation for this is to be found in the philosophical distinction between deductive and inductive reasoning.

3.

Have philosophers found a way to deal with induction that might be helpful to traders whose strategies have been shown to be non-deductive? As is often the case, philosophers have made good ground in elucidating the issues but there is, as yet, little in the way of consensus in terms of a "solution".

The obvious objection to make is that there is no real problem with induction. There are so many instances of seemingly successful inductive arguments and indeed inductive trading strategies with positive profitability, that to doubt induction is plain obstinate. Alas, this argument is unlikely to carry much weight with one who finds induction objectionable, *as it is itself an inductive argument*. Suggesting that many inductive arguments appear adequate and that therefore all inductive arguments are methodologically justifiable or permissible, is quite evidently an inductive argument; from a limited set to a generalisation. Consider a man, whose honesty is in doubt, proclaiming his honesty. His assertion is true if the issue at stake is true. But he is merely asserting the issue at stake. The argument is circular and question begging. Likewise the claim that inductive arguments are *in general* legitimate because so many of them seem to work; it is precisely this *form* of argument that is being questioned.

Karl Popper offered a way of dealing with the problem of induction. We must accept that inductive inference is not deductive and is therefore problematic. However, we can apply deductive reasoning to an inductive inference in that we can prove it to be false. This comes back to the power of the counter-example. A trade may have as its strategy, "Apples always trade at a 10 pence premium to pears, with barely any variance in this number", and this has been inferred from an historic dataset of the prices of apples and pears. Popper suggests that a scientific theory that has been posited cannot be proved by induction, but it can be *disproved* by deduction. In the case of the apples-pears trade, a single instance of say apples trading at a 20 pence discount to pears would destroy the strategy's credibility. We can rely on this move, because it is deductive.

Formally:

Hypothesis: Apples always trade at a 10 pence premium to pears with very little variance.

Observation: Pears are trading at a 20 pence premium to apples.

Conclusion: Apples do not always trade at a 10 pence premium to pears with very little variance.

The observation provides the solitary counter-example needed to disprove the hypothesis. We can now proceed with the conclusion as a new and improved working hypothesis. And furthermore this intellectual *method* is fully justifiable.

However, this seems to present the trader (and indeed the scientist) with more problems than solutions. Primarily, the conclusion is a negative statement, which is certainly less useful for trading purposes. Consider the conclusion from a trader's perspective; there is virtually no simple strategy that suggests itself.[27] Most trades have a positive and specific assertion as their basis, such as the initial hypothesis above. If I suggest it nearly always rains at 3pm on Tuesdays when you intend to go walking, you could take concerted action on this advice, such as buying an umbrella. But if I suggest that it does not always rain at 3pm on Tuesdays when you intend to go walking, this information gives you very little reason to do anything.

Not only is this rather unhelpful for traders, but it also casts science in a fairly bleak light. It suggests science is little more than a sequence of hypotheses which are hung up with no prospect of being proved true, but are merely waiting to be shot down. Worse still, it opens the door for other forms of knowledge acquisition and belief systems to try to claim equal status with scientific methods. After all, the palm reader simply makes a suggestion as to what we might believe about our lives and the world from the 'evidence' as he sees it, and should he be proven mistaken, he can just review his hypothesis like the Popperian scientist in the light of the new information. Eager to distance science from superstition or even plain guesswork, Popper offered the notion of *falsifiability*. The difference between science and other belief systems was the possibility of *disproving* scientific conjectures. The palm reader's erroneous prognostications will never force him to dispel his belief in the practice; if he predicts a happy and long-lived life for somebody who dies in agony soon thereafter, the palm reader can blame a mis-reading of the lines on his own part or claim predictive success in some way by suggesting his forecast was meant in a less literal sense. Happiness and longevity are not precise enough to be argued against in this case, which is convenient for the palm reader.

Popper's ideas are hard to dispute, since the problem of induction is circumvented in some way. But something about his solution seems to run counter to the spirit of scientific endeavour. Science is interested in uncovering truths; general universal laws perhaps, that hold under many or all circumstances. Under Popper, there is no way of knowing when such a law has been found and can be relied upon. So it is not clear how induction has really been avoided. Presumably he may argue that that is not his concern and that he is merely pointing out a logical argument regarding refutation.

Nevertheless, it is worth considering how traders in financial markets fare under Popper, at least in terms of falsifiability. If one accepts that many trading strategies are inductive, can we at least describe their methodology as scientific? I have very grave doubts that we can, regardless of the number of scientists in attendance. A conjecture made by traders on the grounds of inductive inference that becomes a trading strategy will be disproved by the market itself in the form of losses. As a clerk, this was summarily explained to me by a senior trader: "The market corrects arrogance". In this sense at least, the trading strategy or hypothesis is falsifiable. But there are different reasons to doubt that such method is truly scientific. Whilst a trader's hypothesis may be disproved by events in the market, this may be little different to an astrological prediction missing the mark. Being proven wrong is not in itself the mark of correct scientific procedure. It is only arguable that this is the case if the hypothesis has a solid scientific basis in the first instance. And this is highly doubtful, as I shall now argue.

4.

Causation is a tricky philosophical issue. It has concerned thinkers from the earliest times and is largely a metaphysical problem. The philosophy of science has a particular interest in the nature of causation, since its primary goal is often claimed to be explaining what occurs and why, or in other words what causes what and why.

Aristotle posited several types of causation and thought it was largely embedded somehow within the objects concerned. Hume was keener on causation being viewed as a 'constant conjunction' of the sort that meant whenever we witness an event, we always witness a second thereafter; but the cause itself could not be seen as such and there was little more to say about it. Now the issue of causation is bound up with scientific hypotheses, the problem of induction and the existence of so-called laws of nature. Consider witnessing an event A, followed by a second event B, and consider further that this event occurs frequently. The sun sets in the west in the evening and rises in the east the following morning and this sequence repeats, daily. Now one might suggest that the sun's setting *causes* it to rise, if one believes causation is simply a constant conjunction of events. This assertion, recall, is not deductive but inductive, based on a limited set of observations and therefore subject to the general problem of induction. But one might prefer to see causation as a matter of general laws of nature. In this case, one might offer a hypothesis that explains *why* the sun's setting has hitherto always been observed to precede its rising. This hypothesis is intended to reflect an *axiom* that holds true in general. So, one might propose the theory that the sun circumnavigates the earth. This is in contrast to events whose hitherto constant conjunction is mere happenstance; Smith plays the lottery weekly and has always lost for example. There is no law of nature that has ensured Smith has always lost, nor that he always will lose. This is a matter of simple chance and not predictable by employing axiomatic rules.

Now what of the quantitative trading that takes place in the financial markets? It has been suggested that the majority of this trading is not pure arbitrage activity (i.e. built on a deductive set of premises) but so-called statistical arbitrage or inductively grounded. A trading hypothesis is formulated from the observation of sometimes hundreds of thousands of data points. 'Constant conjunctions' are sought. And once a correlative effect is uncovered, bets are placed when a discrepancy in the nature of the conjunction occurs; if one stock lags another with which it is thought to be in some way conjoined then an opportunity is believed to exist. But this hypothesis does not reflect a law of nature. Indeed the hypothesis is simply that the correlation has been observed and will persist. To what extent is this scientific? The answer to this will depend on one's philosophical standpoint. Recall Friedman's criteria for successful method with its emphasis on *predictive* efficacy above all else; stat-arb desks are near-perfect adherents to this rule. But for my part, I find it hard to accept this as being in any way scientific. In proposing a hypothesis that simply describes an observed relationship without an accompanying causal explanation, either the causal mechanism is thought not to matter or it is believed that it can be safely relied upon as an implicitly given fact. This is distinctly unscientific. To be unconcerned as to why something is happening and merely trade on the observation that it does, is profoundly muddle-headed.

To see this, consider the following analogy. Imagine we are seated at a window overlooking the crowds of shoppers on Oxford Street in London. With enough observation, we might to start to notice patterns in the flows of people. Perhaps we see a hand-holding couple who are walking together in one direction. Sometimes they are parted by a group of shoppers walking in the opposite direction, but they always return to each other's side. Now a stat-arb trader noticing this would consider betting (trading) on the fact that they will return to each other whenever they are separated. Their displacement is reckoned in all likelihood to be temporary given the past observations.

Now this may seem a fairly reasonable idea and in practice may prove a successful strategy. One, if pressed, can even suggest a reason why the couple ought to return to one another when partitioned. But this is very different from a *causal* mechanism that dictates that something will happen, in all circumstances, because it is subject to a natural law. There is no such law of nature forcing the couple to walk side by side. If the stat-arb trader sees them part, he will bet on their re-uniting. But there is nothing to stop the couple in reality from splitting up permanently. Perhaps she decides to leave early and go home; there was nothing of this sort in the previously observed activity, so the 'model' of the couple's behaviour cannot possibly be expected to pick up on this new, and radically different, state of affairs. This could not happen if the model and method was genuinely scientific in the sense of attempting to explain a causal mechanism in the world, rather than to merely note frequent occurrences.

Historically, these modelling techniques were strictly limited by the availability of computer processing power and data. As both have since proliferated, the colossal datasets are being mined autonomously by machines looking for correlated events. This is in contrast to earlier modelling which strove to replicate fundamental relationships (more akin to understanding causal links) between say economic variables and company earnings, when the only data available was perhaps end of day closing prices. Now 'tick data' is readily accessible, which provides a data point whenever a stock or instrument trades. This can easily create thousands of data points per day and millions per annum. To a statistician this represents a large sample size at which moment a number of useful theorems might become applicable. For example, the Law of Large Numbers tells us that as one conducts successively more experiments the average result should approach the *expected* value. In simpler terms, the more times one tosses a fair coin, the closer the average *observed* ratio of heads to total tosses will be to the expected value of a half. If one tosses a *large* number of times, the average number of heads to tails should approach the expected value rapidly. So if one observes a relationship between the prices of two equities such that perhaps they approximately move together, one might suppose that since one has tens of thousands of observations, one may invoke the Law of Large Numbers and hence have good reason to believe that the average values for the relationship that one has observed are very accurate reflections of some underlying true values. This is fallacious reasoning on two counts. Firstly, the so-called large number of observations recorded using tick data is only large because of splicing. Consider monitoring the temperature in a garden in degrees Celsius for eight hours. We could take the temperature hourly and have eight observations, half hourly to have sixteen, every quarter hour to generate thirty two etc. And it is likely that there will be some small variation between readings. By checking every second, we could generate 28,800 observations; a 'large' number in terms of statistical sampling. But there is a sense in which this is disingenuous as so much of the data is merely duplication. It is a philosophical argument to suggest that in fact no matter how many observations one makes, the inescapable boundary is that they are made in a solitary day and from a certain frame of reference we have not thousands of observations, but a single one. Secondly, the Law of Large Numbers is only applicable if the observations form a sample from a genuine, stable system. Imagine collecting a sample of values that are the result of a die being cast, but that unbeknownst to us the die is frequently being switched from one loaded die to another, whose expected values are not 3.5 (as per a standard die) but vary between 1 and 6. In this case, the mechanism that is generating the data (i.e. the sequence of throws of various loaded dice) is more complex than we have pre-supposed. In fact, if the switching of the dice is conducted randomly, then there is no prospect of us ever being able to rely upon the distribution of values. Forecasting with any precision would be perilous.

In the case of noticing that the price of two stocks move approximately together, the actual, underlying reason for this observed relationship may be no more robust than in the case of the Oxford Street couple who are thought to walk together *because* they are a couple. Stock prices may move together because they conduct business in the same commercial sector or are of similar size or operate in close geographic proximity or even simply because most people believe they *ought* to move together. But these are categorically not Laws of Nature that must by necessity hold true. This distinction can appear subtle. Its importance is often dismissed by supporters of stat-arb who often claim that the true nature of the relationship is less important than its seeming existence. This again harks back to Friedman's idea of predictive success being paramount in relation to explanatory power. A further claim is sometimes made that it is possible to acknowledge the existence of a true causal mechanism but deny knowledge thereof is accessible or indeed necessary for trading purposes. So, one might remark that a relationship between two instruments has been observed and is profitably tradable but that it is driven by an unknown causal mechanism which need not be understood before the trading strategy is applied.

A recent development along such lines is the attempt to apply artificial neural network theory to financial market data. This is a fascinating instance of sharp, scientific method being put to use without much consideration given as to its appropriateness. The general idea is to create a set of artificial neural networks (often created with random parameters at the outset, to minimise any biasing effect that human intervention might have), which are programmed to mine through immense datasets looking for recursive patterns. They are then allowed to *theoretically* trade on a set of different data using their initial parameters and the patterns they 'believe' they have revealed, from a later time period to see how they would have fared. With enormous computing power available, thousands of such networks can be created, each with different parameters. At the end of the trial the best might be kept, the worst destroyed and another chunk of artificial neural network theory is applied; it is possible to create an artificial *evolutionary* environment that tests the survival fitness of the networks, allows them to adapt and modify, and then re-runs the experiment. So the initial networks are tested for their survival by measuring their potential profit on their trades. Those that make heavy losses will be 'killed off'. The surviving networks then have their parameters modified in some random way, which one can liken to random genetic variation between generations. The procedure is then repeated. The modified networks, 'offspring' of the more successful networks from the generation before, scroll through the data again, seek patterns and then trade theoretically on a second dataset. This process may be repeated *thousands* of times before a (theoretically) immensely successful network or collection of networks has evolved. At this point, the network(s) might be let loose in the real market to trade. From one perspective this is pure pattern recognition (for which purpose artificial neural networks are particularly renowned); it is conceivable that the networks will be trading in the market and the traders monitoring their activity will have no real idea as to *why* the networks are trading as they are. The networks learn to trade from entirely random initial settings; but given the complexity of their evolution and of their tendency to be highly non-linear in the final reckoning, it is extremely difficult to pick out precisely what they are doing and why. The networks that result are typically just a lengthy equation with many terms and cross-terms and parameters devoid of interpretable meaning. There is something undoubtedly impressive about an *artificial* neural network that has learnt to perform a complex task (such as facial recognition) without any human input or teaching whatsoever and by the power of evolutionary forces alone. But the extent to which such machines are uncovering deep underlying truths about a set of data and any causal mechanisms therein, rather than spotting coincidental patterns that happen to continue to exist for some time thereafter (analogous to a long sequence of reds on the roulette wheel) is extremely difficult to ascertain from analysis of the networks themselves.

It is hard to know who is right in this regard or how even to test their claims. For every profitable stat-arb fund smugly professing to profit from statistically observed relationships with no regard for fundamental or causal factors, there are almost certainly many more loss-making rivals. The degree to which the sum of all profits from such trading in the market as a whole, differ significantly from zero is probably impossible to verify. By its nature, this sector of financial markets is particularly covert and secretive. There is often no incentive to disclose details of a winning system. Whilst network servers for the trading strategies will be located close to stock and derivative exchanges and therefore typically in the traditional financial business districts, the traders pressing the 'on' button on these black boxes may purposely be kept away from such places to lessen the likelihood of their conversing with rivals. This is decidedly not a 'people' business.

The extent to which society should be concerned by this algorithmic trading is also hard to gauge. It has been persistently claimed that the extraordinary stock market crash in October 1987 was precipitated by early versions of black box trading systems. The massive increase in their use since that date would certainly be cause for alarm if there is any truth in this suggestion. But at this point, the matter is one more of practical consequence rather than philosophical interest. The more abstract ideas that pertain to stat-arb and similar trading methodologies are concerned with whether the exercise is more than just a variant of the gambler's fallacy; the illogical idea that a sequence of reds on a roulette table is likely to mean a black is due (which is similar in gist to mean-reversion trading) or the equally preposterous belief that a trend is forming and red should continue to be backed (momentum trading). If there is no causal mechanism belying the strategy and no equivalent to a Law of Nature that means the sampled data has been observed for a comprehensible reason, then the strategy is likeable to a gambler's fallacy. No doubt the insights of behavioural economics and psychology would prove helpful in this regard. It is not uncommon for those profiting by dint of good fortune alone to leap to fallacious conclusions, sometimes referred to as *post facto* rationalizing. Winning a raffle, an entirely fortuitous event, will often be explained after the event in some fallacious manner perhaps in consequence of how one's shoelaces were tied or the wearing of lucky underpants that day; that this seems a common, and in many ways natural, human reaction should keep us ever alert to its capacity to mislead. But the metaphysical meaning of a causal mechanism or Law of Nature is not without controversy and judgement as to the validity of statistical arbitrage or algorithmic trading is not a simple matter.

5.

Trading strategies, that are not pure arbitrage, can almost always be reduced to one of two broadly contrary positions. There are trades that profit frequently to a small degree and suffer large losses on rare occasion. The alternative is the direct contrary; small losses on a regular basis with infrequent but large profits. This is likeable to *writing* insurance in the former instance and *buying* insurance in the latter. The writer of an insurance policy collects the insurance premiums until the (unlikely) event occurs, when he suffers considerable payouts (losses). The purchaser of insurance usually expects to forfeit the premium regularly but occasionally the event against which he is insured does indeed occur and he profits greatly from the policy.

It can be very useful, where possible, to reduce trading strategies, often highly complex, to one of these basic profiles. In the case of the financial crisis of 2008, most banks were profiting regularly before this time, for so long as the real estate bubble did not burst. So in this sense they were writers of insurance against this actuality. And it is often the case that banks assume this position, whereas hedge funds and proprietary trading firms, on the whole, take on the contrary. Why this should be so, is a contentious matter. For my part, it has something to do with the short term approach to trading the banks have embraced and the importance given to *annual* results. It stands to reason that traders and bankers beholden to shareholders and AGMs, to annual dividends and annual bonus meetings, will opt to collect the insurance premium (a guaranteed revenue) and hope the unlikely does not happen, rather than pay for a policy (a guaranteed loss) and hope that the unlikely does happen and profits are spectacular. There are many other factors besides; for example bankers operate under the belief that their marginal re-numeration to marginal profitability is rapidly diminishing. In other words, as they or their desks make additional profits, they do not expect that their financial compensation will increase in like proportion. This also serves to dis-incentivise many bankers and traders (perhaps contrary to popular perception) from trying for large windfall profits, which are in many ways commensurable with a safer, longer term play that pays out infrequently but greatly. Some would argue that bankers in fact pursued a strategy which wrote insurance in a leveraged fashion. This aimed to bring about the large payoff associated with the *owning* of insurance, by writing more insurance and collecting more premium than was prudent. This also explains why the losses were so catastrophically large, when the 'unlikely' event occurred. In other words, bankers may have a tendency to adopt positions that are akin to writing insurance, crossing their fingers and hoping for a quiet year. But whilst this guarantees a revenue stream of sorts, it is limited by the amount of insurance that is sold. So traders and bankers, who perhaps are not unduly concerned with their desk, department or firm's survival, might attempt to simply find a way to sell more insurance; by borrowing, by leverage or by the use of derivative instruments.

An instrument or product that when sold generates a small revenue but is accompanied by the risk of a very large, but unlikely, loss, is sometimes referred to as a 'teeny'. The likelihood of a catastrophe is, supposedly, very small or 'teeny'. And there is a saying well known in the derivatives markets that perhaps explains what motivates bankers to assume a position that is likely to be slightly profitable but possibly catastrophically loss-making:

"Sell teenies, to buy Lamborghinis".

6.

Whilst Thales the philosopher made a fortune trading using a cunning derivatives proxy, Sir Isaac Newton lost very large sums in the South Sea stock bubble of 1720, leading him to reportedly declare "I can calculate the movement of the stars, but not the madness of men".

Chapter 5

1.

Bereft of the usual means of paying for his round of drinks, the Babylonian farmer alive in 1785 B.C. was legally entitled to offer as tender, and the landlady of the inn was legally obliged to accept, an amount of corn worth no less than the price of the drinks. If she refused, she would be thrown in the water, in accordance with rule 108 of the Code of Hammurabi.

The Code is an ancient Mesopotamian set of laws literally carved in stone by the edict of the 6th King of Babylon, Hammurabi. The laws cover a variety of likely situations that the King's subjects might encounter in their daily personal, social and commercial lives. It deals with crimes of murder and abduction, but also of corporate negligence; the farmer who let his dams fall into disrepair faced paying reparation if they broke and damaged neighbouring crops through inundation. And if he should be unable to afford the fine he would be liable to enslavement at his victim's hands. Tolerance to robbery was limited; anyone caught in the act faced death.

Now such laws offer an insight into the society of the day, and by considering what might be the theoretical purpose of any such legal framework, this insight is all the richer. Whereas a simple reading of the Code suggests some of the practical problems with which this community was faced in its time, more can be gleaned as pertains to the philosophical and ethical outlook of such peoples if the relationship between law and morality is comprehended.

But this is no simple matter. Contemporary laws often do reflect simple moral principles; murder is often illegal and often considered immoral. But laws can also contrive to make society function more smoothly without obvious moral connotation; Hammurabi's law against the hapless landlady is perhaps one such instance. Refusal to accept the corn as legal tender was, *de jure*, illegal, but the action was not obviously immoral (at least to current observers), unlike say a mass murder. Her subsequent dunking in the Euphrates was perfectly legitimate, but whether moral, immoral or of no moral significance is open to debate.

Debate regarding the financial crisis of 2008, as has been the case in preceding crises, has been conducted in a fog of ignorance. It has become evident that the financial markets and the persons and institutions of which they are constituted are poorly understood in general. The true nature of the entities that exist, the tools in use, and the conceptual edifice upon which trading methodologies have been built, are fully comprehended by no-one, and worse still, the extent of this ignorance is yet to be acknowledged. But these black holes in our knowledge are easily matched in enormity by the bewildering emptiness of what passes for an ethical theory of financial market activity.

To see this, consider the nature of the 'debate' so far (presuming it even merits the name) when set against some of the decided outcomes of the crisis. Firstly some facts; the US taxpayers were asked by Treasury Secretary Henry Paulson for $700 billion (a number allegedly plucked from thin air by Neel Kashkari and then noticed to be approximately 5% of total outstanding commercial and residential mortgages, which thence became the 'justification')[28]. The UK National Audit Office estimated in December 2009 that the UK Government had provided 850 billion pounds sterling of support to the banking system. For comparison, in 2009 the entire budget for Britain's National Health Service was approximately 100 billion pounds. Now regardless of whether these sums are an aggregation of loans, provisional guarantees or direct cash injections, the most basic fact of the matter is that these amounts were deemed necessary to stabilise the system. One may contest that they were grossly overblown and no such genuine liability was ever truly borne by the taxpayer. But this argument relies on hindsight analysis; certainly in the UK, initial estimates as to the necessary provision were too conservative rather than extravagant. Doubtless someone will attempt to make the case in time that no assistance was in reality required, leading to a yet bolder controversialist to suggest the assistance was in point of fact *harmful*. The desire to stand out in the midst of consensus can encourage the original, the outlandish and the ridiculous. And it is easier in hindsight to diminish what were perceived as very great threats, in consequence of their not coming to pass. Financial and economic catastrophe was considered a genuine possibility *at the time* by those in power. Fortunately, there is no requirement on us for present purposes to decide whether state aid was necessary or not; it was deemed necessary by those charged with making such decisions as the ultimate authority, and we can proceed with this apparent fact alone as a premise.

Let us simply accept an exceptional and unprecedented request was made of taxpayers by an industry or was thought by those with whom the final responsibility lies, essential to preserve the financial system's integrity. One might therefore have expected the most strenuous effort to have been made to evaluate the actions and nature of those involved from an ethical and moral perspective. But instead, a cohort of economist, Treasury officials, central bankers and investment bankers simply analysed the problem, decided funds were needed, on the strength of which advice Governments proceeded to write out the cheques. Meanwhile the press and commentators booed almost everyone from the sidelines, frequently resorting to mere name-calling. Governments started to talk of 'irresponsible' rather than 'greedy' bankers and of their having a vague and unspecified 'duty to society', of their addiction to a 'bonus culture' and 'short term speculation'. They even called for 'bankers' to show 'restraint' with regards to bonuses in 2009. Meanwhile, reflecting the weakness of the case made against them, banks offered only the limpest of defences, alluding to their supposed innovativeness and contribution to society at large. Little evidence of note was offered in support of their assertions, and little was called for by a peculiarly unquestioning public.

This event, unparalleled in size and audacity, and seemingly emanating from one industry and a relatively small number of firms, has been met by an almost complete silence as regards the ethics of the matter. Governments seem to have acquiesced to every request made by financiers or advisors (often recent financiers themselves) and apparently hoped the situation would quietly disappear. So keen are the parties to protect their own interest and public perception that no serious, objective moral analysis has even vaguely been attempted. On the rare occasions that a minister or regulator has raised the issue of morality either directly or under some euphemism such as 'social responsibility', they have been swiftly derided by bankers keen to prevent any such dialogue from being initiated or even from other politicians wary of upsetting influential financiers or the institutions that had hitherto filled Treasury coffers via corporate tax takes.

Contrast this with almost any major political event of recent times for the starkness of the juxtaposition to be laid bare. The invasion of Iraq in 2003 was debated fiercely across the globe before and after its occurrence. Of great concern was whether the mission had the necessary moral and legal authority to be conducted. The ethical nature of the decisions that were made was given paramount importance. Now admittedly the decision to go to war is not simply a question of economics; it invariably means people will die. But financial crises, and any economic slumps that result, bring their own measure of misery to millions. The economic recession associated with the banking crisis in 2008 has brought many to the point of destitution. Millions of jobs have been lost. This is no light matter, but one would be mistaken for thinking it so, given the absence of any questioning of the morality of those whose actions are commonly thought to have contributed most to its occurrence.

Why then, is this the case? There is no simple answer but it again surely has something to do with the historic disinterest of philosophers in matters of business coupled with the rapidity with which modern financial markets have emerged in their current, highly complex form. The result from a philosophical perspective is a dark and dangerous void. The nature of the markets and those entities that are active therein are understood but superficially. It is unsurprising then that a full ethical consideration of financial market activity has a corresponding shallowness, as without clearly delineated persons or institutions and a lucid account of their actions, it is hard or impossible to assign moral agency. In other words, until we are happy to say we know *who* is doing what, any normative discussion that suggests what *ought* to be done by *whom* and what not, will be baseless. Any ethical theory must be predicated on a capacity to ascribe moral agency. 'Where there's blame, there's a claim' as certain lawyers suggest. But this is true only in so far as there is a distinct 'someone' to blame.

Cogently determining moral agency is merely the beginning of the matter. It is also necessary to know what actions are being taken by the responsible agents and then, most importantly of all, one must have in view a clear ethical standard or theory by which such actions and agents may be judged.

If one accepts the foregoing discussion that aims to show something of the extant of our ignorance of the nature of financial markets, several things seem to duly follow, as recent experience testifies. In the absence of a thorough understanding of the markets, one might expect uncertainty to follow as to whether or not the markets are a 'good thing'; whether or not the crisis was 'somebody's fault'; whether or not the institutions involved are jointly necessary for the world's economies to function; whether speculation is gambling and whether this is to be welcomed or viewed as an evil; whether greed is good, bankers are greedy, bankers are paragons of virtue/evil etc. etc.

It has been disheartening to see society respond to the crisis by tip-toeing around these issues or burying its head in the sand. This has perhaps been best exemplified by the political classes, whereas the tendency elsewhere has been to resort to caricature and triviality. The Church of England, perhaps in an attempt to assert its moral authority and advertise ethical values it professes to hold dear, roundly condemned certain short stock sellers (as 'bank robbers' according to Archbishop John Sentamu) and denounced various hedge fund activities, but subsequently rather exposed its own muddle-headedness on the matter with its confession to have invested heavily in hedge funds and shorted financial instruments. Further confusion was created by the Church Commission's protestation *against* certain restrictions placed on hedge funds and their investors. But the Anglican Church was certainly not alone in its apparent hypocrisy. Name-calling and unconvincing denunciation against a set of opaque or even-double standards have been the hallmark of society's response to the debacle.

There has been much criticism reserved for regulators and regulation. Former Federal Reserve Chairman Alan Greenspan, who was feted whilst at the helm and as assets bubbled, has seen a swift verdict reversal on his time in office. Thatcherite and Reagonite policies that relaxed regulatory codes have also come under considerable fire (although the systematic programme of de-regulation has been largely undertaken both before and after their eras). Whether any amount of regulation could have prevented the recent disaster whilst allowing markets any modicum of liberty is highly questionable; an exercise in what-if history that is probably of limited value. But given that the recent crisis has seen but a handful of criminal indictments, it does not seem an unreasonable claim to stake that the regulation was in some or many ways inadequate, and perhaps necessarily so.

The lack of an explicit moral compass in financial matters may have explanatory power in this regard. If laws have a role in reflecting our moral conviction, we should be unsurprised when they appear to fail and the resultant eventualities offend our informal moral intuition or sensitivity. Lloyd Blankfein's regrettable comment that his bank was doing "God's work" jars against many people's moral sense. But without a clearer idea as to what banks are indeed doing, it is hard to subject them to any moral test and the laws and regulations, it follows, will fail to encapsulate any ethical behaviour we might like them to explicitly prohibit or implicitly encourage.

What succour can philosophy offer then in this matter? Well, certainly it has an immense back-catalogue whence one might derive inspiration. Ethics has been a major strand of philosophy from Socrates onwards, if not beforehand. The question of how one ought to live one's life has received attention from most of the greatest thinkers in history. Furthermore the ethics of business is an academic branch of study in its own right, although relatively nascent at a few decades old. And as ever, we can expect that financial markets and institutions that participate therein will have peculiarities not found in other businesses or industries for which we must duly account.

By considering a distillation of ethical theory and its history, and the particular issues relating to the financial markets, banks etc. that require due regard, we can begin to outline what the ethics of markets might encompass, and perhaps comprehend the full extent of our current moral callowness.

2.

Philosophy means 'love of wisdom'. But loving wisdom is not synonymous with being wise. It has always struck me, on meeting professional academic philosophers, that their love of wisdom *per se* is often accompanied by decidedly modest claims as to their own personal wisdom (or, of course, a professed ignorance as to the actual meaning of 'wisdom'). Perhaps this is in *faux* emulation of the humble Socratic ideal to only know that one knows nothing? Or perhaps with deep contemplation of the fundamental and abstract comes a genuine realisation as to the limits of our knowledge and our capacity to acquire it? Whatever the truth, the point here is to note that modern philosophers overwhelmingly do not claim to be endowed with greater sagacity than the population as a whole in ethical matters. By the application of philosophical techniques, the philosopher may bring clarity where there has been confusion and a preferred moral path may thereby be illuminated. But this is a distinct procedure from that of say the self-professed wise man who claims to possess a gift of insightfulness or to have the ear of some deity or other. The distinction in practice can be rather subtle; the role of the newspaper 'agony aunt' is to elucidate a situation for an emotionally confounded letter writer, but ultimately it is direct advice that is sought over and above a crisp outlining of the problem. One might optimistically hold that a moral choice made with a rich understanding of the issue at hand, justifies stronger conviction than that of a snap decision made on instinct alone. And whilst this certainly affords a *reason* in hindsight as to how a decision was duly reached, it is no guarantee that the consequences will be morally optimal or right. Regardless of this persistent uncertainty, justification is nevertheless often thought important.

An important distinction that helps place ethics in relation to other philosophical work is that between fact and value, also sometimes presented as the explanatory versus the normative. In earlier chapters, we largely dealt with matters of fact or explanation. When considering the nature of banks or the methodology belying trading strategies, one might reasonably hope that questions pertaining to such matters have objective, factual answers that persistent rational enquiry might uncover. We have techniques to try to discover these truths and furnish ourselves with convincing explanations. But there are matters where it is not certain that factual solutions are discoverable or that they even exist. In certain areas it is far from clear that a binary set of right or wrong answers is appropriate. Most ethical work is classed as normative or value-driven, rather than explanatory or factual. We ask what *ought* one to do, rather than what must one do.

The distinction however is not as fine or precise as to be held as a rigid dividing line between different styles of enquiry. There is overlap in every field of philosophical endeavour; some ethical theories (that their supporters believe are *logically entailed* by their metaphysical and explanatory theories) are held as factual realities. Some metaphysical work questions whether objective facts are even possible at all and therefore suggests that every investigation is merely subjective and normative. But as a working point of difference, the explanatory versus normative framework is a useful mapping of the terrain, albeit with these disputed borders.

Ethics and morality, although used interchangeably for literary variation, do have subtle nuances in meaning. Morality or moral philosophy tends to be more concerned with conduct or the set of rules by which lives are lived, whereas ethical theory has rather more to do with values and the kinds of lives that can or ought to be led. So a moral sense might prevent one from stealing chocolate from the chocolate shop, but this sits in a broader context of how one, ethically, chooses to live one's life.

Now there are challenges that strike at the subject before it has even got going. Questioning the very nature of ethics is, loosely, the role of metaethics. Arguments as to whether ethical discussion has any true meaning, or whether there are ethical solutions that are objective and real, are matters for the metaphysics of ethics, which is called metaethics. These challenges come not just from traditional philosophical points of contention, but also (and increasingly) from proponents of relativism, nihilism, evolutionary psychology, egoism and more besides. This is a fascinating field but for now let us stick with the task at hand, namely to provide a background to ethic philosophy and to see how this relates to the financial markets. To this end, a simplifying assumption will be made, (which is probably less innocuous and more controversial than it may at first glance appear), that ethics and morality are of importance and of relevance when trying to broadly analyse financial markets. It shall be assumed that the subject matter has an ethical face. Note however asserting an ethical aspect is a fairly weak claim, as an ethical framework can encompass many different *moral* systems, including amorality. The assumption really reduces to saying that a discussion regarding financial markets and ethical theory is not, *de facto*, meaningless. It is certainly not a presumption that financial market participants must subscribe to some particular moral code or other.

3.

Ethical theories by and large derive from two principle sources. One is rooted in humanity itself; Protagoras' assertion that *"anthropos metron panton"* or "man is the measure of all things". The force behind humanist ethics is the observation that man differs from other animals in such a manner as to make imperative, moral thinking. It is part of mankind's very essence that he can reason, he is self-aware and he has the capacity to foresee, and this drives him to think *ethically*. To do otherwise would be to emphasize our commonality with animals and to diminish the important and glaring fundamental points of difference between us. The humanist response to those seeking to undermine *every* ethical theory, by denying their authoritativeness or metaphysical status, is to simply posit the existence of ethics as a necessary predicate of humanity. Without ethics, the humanist suggests, humanity is merely synonymous with *homo sapiens*. Now this can be asserted normatively i.e. as a matter of opinion, but the real question is whether it is *logically* the case. But even if this view is simply declared as an article of faith, it is not rendered necessarily worthless in consequence. After all, it claims to be grounded in an understanding of the essence of mankind, which, perhaps less controversially, can at least be claimed to exist.

The like cannot be said for the other historically important source from which moral inspiration has been drawn, namely religion. For perhaps the majority of human history, moral thinking has been dictated by a non-human deity or deities (hereafter, God), often via a self-anointed or supposedly divinely-selected human messenger. Ethical theories attributable in some way to God have influenced human behaviour for all of recorded time. Of course the moral code varies from religion to religion but it derives its authority from God, against which argument there is no logical continuation aside from flat denial. If one accepts the authority, it is naturally reason enough to adopt the prescribed rules of morality, especially as they are often backed up by the threat of eternal suffering in cases of non-compliance. There are two formal logical fallacies at work here; an appeal to authority and an *argumentum ad baculum*. The former tells us to accept the ethics on offer because they come from God, which is only a good reason if God *logically* exists and is without question an authority on ethical matters. The latter tells us to accept the truth of the proposed ethics or else face being tortured for eternity. This is a logical fallacy that appeals to a threatened use of force (*ad baculum* literally translated 'to the stick') against us *which is contingent on the truth of the ethical proposal*. The threat is not simply 'believe in this, or be beaten up'; it is 'you must believe in this because in consequence of its being true, you will be beaten up for disbelieving'.

In the Western world, and certainly where advanced economies and complex financial markets have evolved, these two originating forces have contributed most to the ethical theories of philosophers and the morality that societies have tended to favour. It is necessary to dig deeper however and to see what actual conclusions philosophers and societies have reached in deciding how we ought to live, and indeed to trade.

4.

The story begins, as many do, with Socrates (469-399 B.C.). Prior to him, (and the esteem in which he is held today is indicated by his predecessors' collective nomenclature, the Pre-Socratics), philosophers had concentrated, on the whole, on natural studies. The world, the cosmos and matter were theorized upon; the elements (earth, fire, water, and air), the visible fact of change and the paradoxical idea that nothing in metaphysical reality ever changed at all. When men first began to think in ways now denoted as philosophical, it was with regards to the external physical space in which they found themselves. But Socrates is, rightfully or wrongly, associated with the moment that men began to cogitate introspectively. A separabililily makes itself apparent; there are difficult questions and problems that pertain to men and societies that are unique and seem to exist independently of the natural world *per se*. This was the birth of what is now called the study of the humanities.

What we know of Socrates is from accounts that are second hand, since nothing he wrote, if indeed he did, has survived. We are left nevertheless with a reasonably consistent picture of an ugly man who aroused a great deal of ire amongst the ruling factions. He seems to have been a persistent irritant who claimed, most famously, to have no knowledge himself, saving that he knew himself to be ignorant. It is not hard to see how he became so unpopular, as he was a famed interlocutor who would take to task anyone who claimed to know anything with certainty, but always from his own position of professed complete naïveté. Socrates would then proceed to undo his opponent by making him expose the contradictions and fallibilities in his firmly held belief *for himself.* One might well go out of one's way to avoid Socrates; he is beyond reproach since he claims no point of view on any matter, but still leads one to undermine oneself. Finally, the authorities lost patience with this subtly subversive approach and trumped up charges against him suggesting he was corrupting the youth of Athens. He was condemned to death by self-administered hemlock.

We are left with a handful of aphorisms or sayings attributed to him, such as his reaction to the market stalls "Look at all these things I don't need" or that "A man can tell you precisely how many sheep he has, but not how many friends" for example. But more importantly, Socrates left unanswered questions. What is good? What is the good life? What is virtue? He left more besides, providing an idealist's model for the free thinking and doggedly questioning philosopher, a martyr to the cause of reason and the attainment of wisdom. Socrates is the father of the humanities, the successive phases of human enlightenment and by the manner of his death, of romanticism. Claiming lineage of thought from the Socratic paragon has been an appeal to authority carrying weight ever since.

The quest to find the highest good in life (or *summum bonum*) was taken up with greatest gusto by Socrates' pupil Plato, and in turn by Aristotle. The ethical writings of Plato are not as easily isolated as Aristotle's; the latter wrote recognisable treatises on ethics (in particular the Eudemian Ethics and the Nicomachean Ethics), both highly accessible works. This fact perhaps contributes to their having been adopted as central to scholastic and academic ethical curricula for almost two millennia. Plato's ethics however are more tightly interwoven with his political, metaphysical and epistemological works and he probably felt this inseparability was unavoidable. Omitting dozens of important thinkers aside from these two giants, the most important ethical theories thereafter, and before Christian hegemony arose in the middle of the first millennium A.D., are those of the Cynics (and specifically Diogenes of Sinope) and the vaguely descendant ideas of Stoicism and Epicureanism.

This crudely outlines the chief ethical theorists or schools of thought from Socrates' death in 399 B.C. to Constantine's adoption of Christianity as the official religion of the Roman Empire in 313 A.D. The moral code inspired by the revelation of Jesus of Nazareth, and hard-coded by St Paul, broke decisively away from the Classical past in many ways, not least in externalising its metaphysical foundations away from mankind to a remote omnipotent God. The search for the highest good was duly considered a closed case by believers and ecclesiastical thinkers; all that was left was to propagate seeds of faith and religiosity whilst exterminating heresy and apparent falsehoods. The writings of Plato were selectively incorporated into Christian doctrine and those of Aristotle were likewise (most enthusiastically by Thomas Aquinas in the mid-13th century) adopted, where apposite.

This reflected an admiration for thinkers who, in the Church's eyes, had partially grasped Christ's Revelation before His arrival. Where Stoicism chimed with Church orthodoxy, it too was acknowledged. Epicureanism, a doctrine roughly soliciting pleasure in preference to pain, was strictly off-message from a Christian standpoint. Its misfortune to become inextricably associated with licentiousness (which is a most inaccurate portrayal) only served to confirm its perceived heretical nature. The Cynicism of Diogenes has much in common with Jesus' outlook, although the habit of the former to masturbate in public is not one which the Gospel's record the latter as imitating, and may explain the Church's reluctance to highlight any shared moral values between the two. Diogenes was the son of a banker in Sinope and became one himself, but following an obscure financial scandal he repudiated the notion that worldly possessions were requisite for a happy life, moved to Athens and lived much like a stray dog, in a barrel. He reputedly wandered the streets with a torch in the daytime "seeking an honest man". As in Jesus' case, Diogenes actions spoke as loudly as his words and influenced many thinkers to come, whilst also in parallel to Jesus, few would take him literally at his words and live in the abject poverty advocated.

Ethical theories of religious origin are rooted in how one should live this life to win approval from an invisible Deity, who will reward or punish judiciously on death with consequences that will last for all eternity. The ethics of antiquity, whilst not unanimously discounting the possibility of an immortal soul or afterlife, tend instead to enquire as to how to live well in this life *for its own sake*. Ethical theories guided by humanist sentiment can, very approximately be cast into three lots. How one ought to live so that one lives a *good* life is the approach to moral philosophy known as *virtue ethics*. The ethicists of ancient Greece largely concurred that this was the basis of ethics; they differed markedly however in their various accounts of what was meant by a virtuous or good life. For Epicurus, the good life was one of pleasure and an absence of pain; for the Stoics, it was a life lived in accordance with nature; for Plato, a life of contemplation of the true nature of things and so on and so forth. These are of course simplifications of their philosophical ideas, but for now the point to note for when the time comes to attempt to apply these systems to the financial markets, is that the broad methodology employed is to cast ethics as an account of how one ought to live, so as to live virtuously.

The two other predominant branches of humanist ethics are known variously as on one hand deontological, duty or rights-based ethics, and on the other as consequentialist ethics. The former emerges strongly from the Renaissance, when men began to reacquaint themselves with humanist ideas. Initially they did so within the old religious confines, but later, as the Reformation, libertarianism and science loosened the Church's grip, in the context of an ethical framework measured once again by man rather than God. When moral thinking re-focussed itself in this way and as men realised that through science and Enlightened reasoning the laws that governed the physical world could be understood and made to serve their own purpose and fancy, confidence was restored and God made superfluous. This would last for half a millennium until the horrors of 20th century global warfare brought metaethical concerns to the fore once again. But to the early modern humanists, man's capacity to become enlightened marked him out as special, to which end, they concluded, he is born with certain rights.

Now the supposition that men are born with rights, (which in relative terms is a fairly recent conceptual notion), almost automatically leads to a moral theory. For in so far as I am born with rights, they only have meaning if others are duty bound to respect them. So in essence, ethical theories based on the existence of natural rights are theories of *obligation*. If we are happy to accept, say, the right to freedom of belief, then the real relevance or onus of the right is not so much to or on the holder but to or on those with whom he interacts. It is not hard to see where such theories might run into difficulties; rights may directly conflict or fail to attain universal acceptance. Unless a right is logically deduced from some set of true assumptions, its justification may always be a matter for dispute.

The final types of ethical theories, which emerged most starkly from utilitarian thinkers of the 19th century, are known generally as consequentialist. Here, the idea is that our actions should be guided by their outcomes or consequences. In the Utilitarian variant of consequentialism the rule was to do anything that would contribute to achieving the greatest happiness for the greatest number. So, to make the obvious contrast with rights-based ethics, it could well be morally admissible to violate one person's rights if that increased the overall tally of happiness for society as a whole, whereas the rights-ethicist would stand for no such action since rights are classed as inviolable. In the words of Ronald Dworkin, "Rights are trumps", but then again in the words of Utilitarianist Jeremy Bentham, "Rights are nonsense on stilts".

It is worth highlighting a fundamental point of difference at this juncture. Kant had a notion of a Kingdom of Ends, whereby a guiding moral principal of people's actions was that no-one else should be treated simply as a means to an end, but always as an end *in themselves*. People have a right not to be used purely instrumentally, however well-intentioned the user may be. This line of thought is in direct conflict with some consequentialist prescriptions of behaviour; utilitarians might advise that using someone purely as a means (say by heavily taxing their annual bonuses) is not only desirable but is perfectly just and moral conduct.

One might be forgiven for thinking at first glance that this account of the history of ethical theory is rather theoretical and of little to no importance in practical reality. This can often *appear* to be the case when the abstracting and clinical hand of philosophy is turned to the prosaic and routine; the familiar with which one feels comfortable, suddenly seems remote and hypothetical. Whilst perhaps an understandable sentiment, this is both unwelcome and limiting. It is at the heart of philosophical enquiry to seek out the true nature and structure of everything that surrounds us and every complex situation we perceive, and this must entail a generality of thought that is not contingent upon particulars. However, once a non-specific logical model is formulated, it is often with reference to the specific, to the mundane and to familiar experience that it is tested.

Furthermore, it becomes easy to think of philosophy or perhaps even philosophers as distinct from society in some way. Sadly, this suggestion is not entirely without grounds, as contemporary professional, academic philosophers largely inhabit a technical and esoteric world of their own creation, publishing for a handful of fellow academics on the minutiae of minutiae. The oft-levelled criticism that there is little if any practical benefit to such effort is somewhat misguided, since applications derived from knowledge are rarely anticipated before the knowledge is acquired: we do not research pure mathematics or theoretical astrophysics only in so far as we can see specific practical reasons for so doing. Our theoretical understanding may run years or decades ahead of obvious actual application. Nevertheless, the current insistence by central government that academics publish incessantly would seem a recipe for papers marginal and incremental to existent theory, rather than the radical, perpendicular jolts of inspired thought that every subject needs now and again to evolve and which may take many years to mull over without interruption.

Yet from the time of Socrates until at least the mid 20th century, philosophers and their work on ethics were inseparable from their contemporary societies. The history of civilized mankind is entirely intertwined with the history of philosophical ethics. The ethics of Plato and of Aristotle are bound up in the democratic, yet slave-owning, society in which they lived. Stoicism was the quasi-religious moral code guiding personal conduct throughout much of the Roman Empire for half a millennium, so much so that an Emperor, Marcus Aurelius, became one of its most celebrated adherents and proponents. How can one make sense of human history and activity in the so-called Dark to Middle Ages without reference to Christian morality and the authority of the Church in ethical matters? From whence did the Constitution of the United States of America emerge, if not from Enlightened thinkers such as Paine, Montesque, Locke, Diderot, Rousseau and Franklin? And how are re-distributive taxes (which some argue are the mere confiscation of legitimate property from one for the intended benefit of another) justified morally in our own time if not by consequentialist arguments that the resultant state of affairs is preferable in some way?

So very loosely then, we have four principal types of ethical theory, which are certainly not entirely distinct and independent and have influenced one another at various times in history. But essentially we have theories based on some understanding of what is meant by a good or virtuous life (virtue ethics), theories of religious origination, theories predicated on the existence of rights, duties and incumbent obligations (deontological ethics) and finally theories that designate actions as moral in the light of their consequences (consequentialist ethics).

And in actuality, if we live by any moral compass at all, it usually involves a conglomeration of such ideas. The historic balances between liberty and authority, left and right, socialism and capitalism, have corresponding claims and counter-claims for and against their associated ethical outlooks. The free market entrepreneur claims his right to trade without interference from authorities and in accordance with his conception of the good, virtuous and successful life. He may claim the consequences of his endeavours are also worthy, creating wealth and opportunity for others. And perhaps he fixes the roof of the local Parish church and seems to have every moral base covered by every type of ethical system. But then his right to trade so freely is challenged by someone denying this right, *per se*, and by another who claims to have a conflicting right, perhaps not to suffer from the externalities of the business. Another questions why the trader thinks living as he does is necessarily so virtuous and appeals to a different vision of the good life. And then questions arise as to whether a much better outcome for society as a whole could be achieved by heavily taxing the trader or even prohibiting his activity entirely.

Such is the general idea. None of the moral philosophies has made so compelling a case as to have theoretical hegemony. In practice, hegemony of religious morality has been common, for example under the theocratic rule of the various Islamic caliphates. In Grecian antiquity virtue ethics were given great prominence, but no one particular strain dominated. Stoicism enjoyed favouritism under Roman rule and has experienced several revivals since the Renaissance, even from Christian humanists.

Now whilst it is said that none has made so undeniable an argument as to dominate moral philosophical thinking, many ethical theorists do believe that their system is not merely subjective opinion but the outcome of an objective, metaphysical reality. In other words, they do not simply suggest a moral theory that they suppose we might like to consider adhering to, but press a far stronger claim that theirs is a *logically derivable* scheme demanding compulsion. So Kant believed that his conception of an ethical life was a logical outcome of his theories about the reality of the world and that there were objective standards against which behaviour was measurable. This made pursuing the correct course of action *categorically imperative*, in his phrasing.

In many ways this is the flip side to the still-fashionable, but for some lamentable, notion of the morality of relativism. In its purest form, this states that there are no objective standards of behaviour; every moral code has equal validity in the relativist's sight. There is a tendency for this to be confused with an entirely different ethical viewpoint, namely that of tolerance. To tolerate is to accept the actions of others in so far as they do not conflict unreasonably with one's own ethics, whereas to be a relativist is to have complete indifference to the moral conduct of others. The conflation of relativism with tolerance is often a scourge on ethical debate, as relativism renders all such debate instantly futile. (It is also, incidentally, self-defeating in one sense, since it is an *absolutely* held position; if one believes firmly that all ethical theories are of equal worth, then this is an absolutist, not relativist, position and, *ergo*, an hypocrisy).

Now that the landscape of moral philosophy has been mapped out, if but sketchily, we can ask what in the way of moral guidance have we inherited from past thinkers with respect to matters of finance, commerce and wealth? Can we apply ethical theories formulated so many centuries before credit default swapping was a life-style choice? Let us see firstly what can be gleaned directly from the past before we are forced to advance our own suppositions.

5.

The pickings are really rather slim. Boiling down 2,500 years of moral philosophy to a few base elements hardly seems to do justice to the wonderful array of compounded ideas. Yet some generalizations do stand up to methodological scrutiny; for instance the dominance of Christian theological morality in the Western world from circa 300 A.D. to 1300 A.D. meant an over-arching ethic was, at least in theory, widely accepted with regards to wealth and commerce, and it does not seem unreasonable to emphasize this particular prescription given its scope. The ethical standpoint promulgated by Jesus in the Gospels and reiterated in the Middle Ages (when it appeared for practical expedience's sake to have been forgotten by the Church) by St Francis of Assisi in particular, was the utter renunciation of wealth and riches in favour of a life of near-total impoverishment. Jesus' message is unequivocal, "Lay not up for yourselves treasures upon earth..." (Matthew 6:19), "Therefore take no thought, saying, What shall we eat? Or What shall we drink? Or Wherewithal shall we be clothed?" (Matthew 6:31), "Give to every man that asketh of thee, and of him that taketh away thy goods ask them not again" (Luke, 6:30). The message really is very consistent and insistent; give your wealth away to the poor. All of it.

Grey- and black-friars aside[29], it is not an easy matter to find widespread, literal adherence to this rule, even when and where Christianity was the foremost authority on ethical matters. In its pre-eminent heyday, economies stuttered along as very low-output pre-industrialised agri-feudalistic affairs. Poverty was not so much optional but rather unavoidable for the vast majority of the laity. And the solace afforded to the poor by the Gospel message must surely be offset in some measure against its crushing effect on entrepreneurial ambition. Consider the following lifestyle options for the peasant of the Dark or Middle Ages:

1. Work harder to accrue capital that generates further wealth of its own accord, and find it very hard to enter Heaven or risk spending an eternity in Hell,

or

2. Sit back, put up with the hunger, wait for the plague or another incurable disease and enjoy an eternity of Divine bliss.

This 'dilemma', presented admittedly somewhat flippantly, was of the utmost seriousness to people for a great slice of recorded history. Of course, there was little real choice to make; even if the first option was feasible, and often it was not, the selection really came down to heaven or hell. The third way of course, was to work harder, accrue wealth and give it all away. But given that this had the same payoff as 'do nothing' and carried the added risk that the lightning bolt would strike *before* the great acts of philanthropy had occurred, this strategy, in game theoretic parlance, is *dominated* by the second option under all circumstances and is therefore not a rational option. It would not be until the Protestant Reformation that a way was found to twist logic sufficiently so as to make working very hard and accruing no wealth morally *preferable* to working minimally and accruing no wealth.

Pre-Christian ethics were, as has been discussed, more concerned with living a good life for its own sake, than with living so as to please an external God. So what role did wealth and trade have to play? Here matters are greatly more complicated than in the case of the Christian era. Consistency is not assured and generalization is more perilous. The Cynics espoused a view closely resembling Jesus', that wealth and possessions carried no meaning and contributed nothing to, or worse perhaps hindered, the quest for the *summum bonum*. Others were less condemnatory with regards to materialism. The Stoics, or at least those of the later, Latinized variety, ranked wealth as a 'preferred-indifferent', which is to say that riches were neither necessary for happiness or a good moral life nor, perhaps obviously, were they sufficient, but they could certainly still be preferable to the alternative (poverty) without contradiction. Early Stoics were less equivocal about the matter; they had an expressed admiration for the self-sufficiency of Diogenes the Cynic, tempered only by a pragmatic acknowledgement that to live with some means and in some material comfort was likely preferable to complete impoverishment. Gradations of 'indifference' were a later development in Stoicism; earlier versions preferred a simpler separation of the essential from the inessential. Whilst Epicureans also rejected the Cynics' disdain for all worldly goods, their conception of the good life being one without pain and full of pleasure is not necessarily associated with materialism. The followers of Epicurus saw a distinction between mental and physical pleasures and pain. The greatest happiness was tranquillity resulting from an absence of mental anguish. Physical and mental pleasures were definitely to be welcomed. But by living a philosophical life, with a good circle of friends and seeking wisdom, the fear of death could be overcome and mental strife avoided. Epicurus and his disciples lived in a commune and feasted once a month; everything in moderation, even moderation. It is hard not to avoid comparison with hippy communes, which if valid, gives an insight into their view of commerce and wealth; in a word, indifference.

Within the ethical theories of Plato and Aristotle it is important to maintain context, specifically the very close relationship between the individual and society. Plato spells out in the *Republic* a just, hypothetical society with citizens individually living in accordance with the cardinal virtues.[30] The egoism of later theorizers such as Epicurus is far less apparent. Suffice to say that the good life is (yet again and perhaps unsurprisingly) a life contemplating the nature of the virtues and living the life one ought to live. This latter point seems question begging or circular (since how one ought to live is the very matter at hand), but essentially in the virtuous city Plato envisages, ruled by Philosopher Kings, everyone follows their own vocation such that, say, a soldier lives the life of a just soldier, and all is as it should be. The role of wealth and commerce in this utopian vision is almost negligible. Plato sees the value of wealth or the economic output of workers and auxiliary artisans as necessary but only to the extent that they are strictly so. Over-indulgence of any sort in everyday pleasures or functions is solidly inferior to time spent philosophizing, contemplating the ideal and true.

Less ascetic and, some might suggest, less irritating than Plato's paragon of virtue, is Aristotle's virtuous man.[31] Aristotle professes a moral instruction aimed at the attainment of 'eudaimonia' which is translated as 'happiness' but reluctantly so, since 'happiness' in contemporary usage has a rather more shallow and temporary nature that inadequately expresses what is intended. The *summum bonum* of Aristotelian thought is not happiness of the sort resulting from a good night out or a small win at the races. It is the fulfilment of a life of contented and virtuous being. This is not necessarily a life of pleasure, but one of courage, knowledge and justice. Both Aristotle and Plato place great emphasis on the love we (consequently) call Platonic, between friends.

So the classical thinkers leave us a little in the dark. If they discussed commercial life at all, it was often either to condemn it as frivolous or irrelevant, or worse as un-virtuous. In defining the good life, the highest good or the virtues, it is impossible to find much that relates directly to matters of finance or trade. Two caveats here; firstly of the massive pool of slave labour in antiquity we must be ever mindful. Plato's philosophical dreamer (hypothetical or not) in his ivory tower would be furnished with life's necessities and saved the trouble of their procurement only through an economic arrangement of enslavement. Secondly, we can hardly expect to read Epictetus or Lucretius and find direct moral guidance on collateralized debt instruments. This point may seem facile, yet some would have us dismiss ancient insight out of hand on this very score. But this is irrational and short-sighted. It is in consequence of their attempting to find the ultimate nature of an ethical life that philosophers avoid overt emphasis on quotidian trivialities or particular societal attributes of their own time. Whilst extracting themselves from their immediate surroundings is, *de facto*, impossible, in so striving they aim to give their resultant theories timelessness reflective of the truths they purport to uncover. Therefore, to level a criticism of irrelevance or out-datedness is really to miss the point. It is left for us to calculate their response to our problems, by use of our reasoning and the guidance of their writings.

As to later, post-Christian ethicists, we find general laws of morality from deontological thinkers; perhaps most famously Kant's imperatives to treat others not merely as means but always as an end in themselves and to act in such manner that one would happily will such behaviour to be *universally* replicated. This chimes with the so-called Golden Rule of morality, prevalent in almost all religious instruction, to treat others as one would wish to be treated. This 'coincidence' was a happy one for Kant who remained a Christian throughout his life. From consequentialists, we receive a clearly conflicting notion that we should value successful ends above all else; the means of their achievement are subordinated.

The debate between these two major branches of ethical philosophy largely dominates contemporary political and social moral discourse. The legacy of Christian morality is far from negligible but the pagan ethics of virtue, 'manliness' or even Homeric heroism are deeply unfashionable and in the main neglected. They have been reduced to a rump of trite one-liners about 'money not bringing happiness' or 'a friend in need...' etc. fit only for greetings cards. Furthermore the curse of nullifying relativism has struck, which only serves to stifle assertions that a good life consists in any specific action or way of living. This, I contest, is a great pity for reasons that should become clear. When well-intentioned consequentialists bump up against the rights of individuals that some consider sacrosanct (an unstoppable force meeting an immovable object), a dash of Stoic manners or Aristotelian courage and magnanimity may not go amiss in seeking a resolution, and this is certainly more proactive than the relativist's shoulder shrugging.

In short, we will have to work harder to find the answers we seek. But it should now be clear that the very tentative moral claims that have been staked since the crisis of 2008 can be traced back to their theoretical roots, although of this the claimants may well be unaware. So when politicians claim banks have a duty to lend to business and not simply engage in speculation for their own account, they are making a deontological ethical claim. When hedge funds justify their strategies with respect to the large amount of corporate taxation they pay, they are providing a consequentialist argument as moral justification for their activity. Hopefully it is clear not only to which broad ethical theory such claims can be attached, but how these different branches of ethical philosophy line up in relation to one another. This leaves just one important question. Who is right?

Chapter 6

1.

On 13 September, 1970 an article appeared in the New York Times Magazine entitled '*The Social Responsibility of Business is to Increase its Profits*' and its author was Milton Friedman. A typically pithy piece of scholarship, it argues, in only a few thousand words, for a classical, free market understanding of the relations between business, society and ethics. It presents solutions to many of the difficult questions that confront us and explicitly or otherwise fixes parameters that envelop the debate. And since Friedman was something of a purist and his position is helpfully located at one end of a spectrum, it makes for a very useful benchmark.

He argues that a business cannot have social responsibilities since it is not a person, and only persons may have responsibilities. Ignoring for now the obvious fact that this contradicts the article's title, this sets an important boundary for commerce or business as a whole in its relation to society. Friedman does weaken his argument somewhat when he drops to the level of the corporation which 'is an artificial person and in this sense may have artificial responsibilities'. He goes on to ask what these supposed social responsibilities, that are often thought to exist, imply and for whom? He presumes the 'to whom' are businessmen and, specifically, corporate executives, as those workers of lowlier status really have very little decision-making powers to hand. Friedman then employs the neat distinction, well-worn in the economic academic wardrobe, between agents and principals. Now although the executive is a powerful figure who makes vital decisions regarding the business' activities, he does so solely in his role as an agent, acting on behalf of the principal(s) i.e. the owners of the firm.

So the executive has responsibility as an agent to his employer alone. If he should make corporate decisions that are not *entirely* focussed on enhancing profits due to the capital-holders, but instead pursue social objectives to his own liking, he ceases to act merely as an agent for the corporation but as a self-appointed social agent. The moment that the executive makes a decision to allocate resources without a fully concerted profitable motive, he is effectively taxing either the owners or the customers (if say he raises prices to raise revenue to spend socially rather than to invest). This, argues Friedman, is socialism, not free-market capitalism.

Now he recognises that the owners may well wish to spend their profits on charitable works or creating schools or hospitals. But that is their choice as principals. The corporate executive may do likewise but only on his own time and with his private funds. Another distinction then follows; leisure (or principal) time and company (or agent) time. Finally, Friedman argues not only is this all the case ethically, but, if followed as a code of conduct, the outcome is likely to be more efficient that the alternative whereby corporate executives try to achieve some vague social goal such as 'fight inflation', which will necessarily be a messy and slipshod affair.

Before considering the merits of Friedman's implied theoretical ethical theory, and attempting to apply this to the financial markets in particular, let us consider the meta-ethical framework that he has constructed. Firstly Friedman is discussing the key topic of moral agency with which our discussion on ethics largely began. He is considering with whom or on what responsibilities rest or fall. This process of assignation is critical in ethical debates; it is a relatively simple matter to determine agency at the level of individual persons, say in the case of a father and his child or a robber and his victim. But the waters quickly muddy when groupings or social collectives are implicated. The responsibilities due to a company, an army or a nation are immediately contentious because of the ontological issues surrounding the nature of a group that is constituted by individuals.

Can any grouping have moral agency or accountability? Our intuition might suggest as much, but when one attempts to analyse the group philosophically, it is harder to be so certain. Are members of a group collectively and jointly responsible or individually and partially responsible? Is the responsibility separable amongst the members? Asserting that a bank is responsible for an action is only meaningful if the means by which a bank can have agency and can be identified is clear. In 'blaming' a bank or the financial industry, what precisely are we doing? These are enormously difficult questions that have occupied philosophers extensively in ethics generally. But Friedman's article offers a particularly neat exit strategy from the conundrum. Corporations, as entities, have no real responsibility at all, since they are artificial constructs. Employees have responsibility solely towards their capital-owning employers and then only to maximise profit. Capital holders have no social responsibility in relation to their capital stock above and beyond what the law dictates. Everyone is duty bound not to break any laws and "engage in open and free competition without deception or fraud".

This really is rather useful. Not only has Friedman identified the moral agents (and as importantly excluded agents and entities to which no responsibilities ought to be assigned) but furthermore he makes clear the extent of the duties and obligations incumbent on the players concerned. As agents, these are to maximise the return on capital as an employee, subject to an obeisance of the laws. As to principals (which is capital-owners at all times and workers in their leisure time), the theory passes little comment and this is entirely consistent. The model is one of business ethics and as Friedman does not recognise the business entity as having responsibilities, matters are greatly simplified. The responsibilities that the capital owners (or employees outside of work) have to society are extraneous and exogenous to his model.

Friedman's theory of business ethics is not of course the only such proposal. The philosophy of business ethics has an academic pedigree albeit barely decades old. Also, we must be aware that the particular branch of business with which we are concerned, namely the financial markets, has elements rendering it distinct from other business, and the applicability of much of the literature will therefore be contentious. Added to this has been a tendency amongst philosophers to re-cast the issues in the philosophy of business as directly analogous to those of political philosophy, which allows for the interminable re-hashing of arguments between old foes from the left and right. There has also been a tilt towards issues that have perhaps more obvious ethical connotations in commerce such as the use of cheap overseas labour, the encouragement of 'brain-drains' from less developed nations to more developed etc. Until the monumental events leading up to 2008 it was probably not obvious to many that matters of ethics were of much importance with respect to financial market activity and its relation to society. Indeed, to an obtuse many this is still not apparent.

For in raising these matters with many, many traders and bankers over the years, the most common word I have heard used in conjunction with the relationship between morality and the markets is 'irrelevance'. And it is for this reason that I consider Friedman's article of paramount importance, since it is a startlingly accurate reflection of what counts for an ethical code amongst the majority of financial market participants. Of course few are as forthright in their conviction, at least publicly, as Friedman. But the *ad hoc*, token acceptances by banks that they realise they have a societal duty ring hollow for good reason; it is patently clear that the banks do not believe this themselves, judged by their actions. Nor, furthermore, is it apparent that a compelling case has been made against Friedman's assertions in order to demonstrate that such duties do in fact exist.

Such is the dreadful shallowness of what has passed for a debate. We recognise that banks and other financial institutions are critical to the functioning of modern economies, or perhaps more pertinently, we fear this to be true to such an extent that we are not prepared to allow them to fail, lest we be proven right and the consequences calamitous.

So, vital or not, the result is much the same; we will not let banks fail *collectively*. And yet, we seem entirely loathe to consider this a compelling situation in need of serious ethical consideration. Banks, financial firms and workers in the industry seem disinterested in such matters, but more surprisingly so too do politicians, thinkers and taxpayers. The basest instinct surfaced in reaction to the crisis, namely vengeance, and the effect has been to skew the debate away from what ought to be its true focus. A process that should examine the ethics of finance from first principals, and as generally as possible, has been pivoted upon the remuneration of bankers and, specifically, bonus payments. This is akin to only having interest in a wrong-doer forfeiting the material proceeds of their activity, whilst paying scant regard for the act and its own significance. This is an unusual manner in which to proceed; in the case of those deemed actively criminal, it is the crimes themselves that primarily concern society and rarely just the value of ill-gotten gains. It is the crime that is punished and sentencing tends to reflect the perceived gravity of the offence rather than the value of the utility the criminal sought to gain. This is not to suggest that bankers or traders acted criminally; there has been a marked absence of evidence as to that (which some would construe as all the more disconcerting). Yet an intuitive sense that something *immoral* occurred is not uncommonly felt; a feeling that certain financiers have amassed vast ill-deserved fortunes whilst causing grief and misery elsewhere in the economy.

Friedman's article is provocative but its theoretical, normative claims about appropriate behaviour bear striking resemblance to the actual workings of the financial markets. The alacrity for bonus super-taxing has been accompanied in some cases by plaintive requests for evidence of contrition on the part of bankers; for proof that they 'realise what they have done'. Such cries have met with cold silence, but if one presumes that Friedman's model is a good fit for reality, it is perfectly simple to see why this should be the case. Bankers, traders, brokers and analysts do not feel contrite individually or collectively because they do not assign any moral agency to themselves, beyond that with respect to their employer. Friedman's ethic has the consequence of absolving the market participants from any social responsibility whatsoever. Stockholders are at liberty to pursue any social ambitions they choose, subject to law. And workers, from lowly administrators to power-crazed Chief Executives, have but one aim and duty: to increase the return to capital. This then is the ethical philosophy of financial markets, *as adopted by the participants themselves*. But what is more, it has received tacit agreement from the rest of society. This is partially reflected in the laws and regulations which did not attempt to encourage alternative behaviour before the crisis but also in the feebleness of attempts since to even provoke a morality-centred discussion.

How then to proceed? Firstly, an acknowledgement of the *status quo* is important. The ethic of business advocated by Milton Friedman has been, consciously or otherwise, assumed in almost every detail by those in the financial markets. And society has made little concerted effort to interfere where it might be expected to object. The evidence for this being the state of affairs is considerable; from the refusal of any banker or trader to accept responsibility for the crisis to the wishy-washy claims that banks have certain, unspecific duties because of their very nature. The nature of banks, as discussed earlier, is highly complex and ill-understood. But as to their having certain intrinsic duties to society, this assertion requires a sophisticated ethical explication, detailing from whence such duties arise, what precisely they entail and in what sense they are binding. I know of no such coherent, cogent or compelling argument. So continuing with the assumption of a Friedmanite ethic as being all-pervasive in the markets leads naturally enough to certain questions. Is this a desirable or optimal or justifiable situation? Is there a more preferable alternative arrangement?

Relating this ethic back to the philosophical roots discussed in the previous chapter is helpful. Of course, Friedman's ideas do not sit well with Christian morality. The two are evidently juxtaposed and beyond reconciliation.[32] With that in mind, let us exclude Christian theological morality henceforth; only by entering every dealing room in London, New York and elsewhere and upturning every desk are we likely to act in complete accordance with its tenets. I do not believe this would be sensible; at least not for *every* desk.

Friedman's business morality is clearly deontological, which is to say based on the notion of rights and duties. The guiding principle of every market participant is that he should fulfil his obligation to his employer by maximising profit. Pursuing any other goal is an abuse of one's position as an agent since one ceases to act in the best interest of the principal. The moral rectitude of an action is measurable against its profitability and legality. It is the right of capital holders that employees should act thus.

It is dutifulness that underpins this philosophy of business ethics. And Friedman also believes this to be not only just but likely to render the resulting situation in some sense optimal. However it is too great a reach to consider the theory consequentialist; the derivatives trader should not be looking to trade as profitably as possible because the aggregate outcome in the economy and society will be an efficient distribution of resources. This ought not to be his primary motivation, but it is a happy by-product of the system as a whole, according to Friedman, the free-marketeer.

Now ethical theories often rub together tectonically; in following a consequentialist programme of reducing the risks associated with terrorist attacks, one might argue for the power to over-ride certain personal liberties such as *habeas corpus*. A confliction occurs and something must give. But in the case of Friedmanite business ethics, which I argue to be tacitly accepted as a norm in the financial markets, rights and agency are clearly enunciated and purportedly without being contrary to consequentialist ethical ideas, since the outcome has an inherent optimality. And arguments along these lines have consistently been offered by senior bankers when faced with criticism; society as whole is as well off as it can be under the arrangement as it stands.

The objection to this is obvious. Either the recent disaster was the best that could be hoped for and all part of an optimal set-up, or the system was not truly functioning on Friedmanite lines or the ethic is flawed. Those who claim that the crisis was part of an optimal free-market capitalist system or that the system was not purely capitalist enough, are little different from 20th century Marxists who continually defended the theory but bemoaned the supposedly botched implementation and explained away serious short-term set-backs as necessary pain before the gain. It should be clear that the backdrop to the credit crisis was one of very light touch regulation and near unrestricted flow of capital. Therefore provocative *laissex-faire* assertions that the problem was the result of overly *constricted* markets surely prove their theories un-falsifiable and thereby, arguably non-theories.

Now one could contest the ethic's ascription of agency or the duties incumbent. So one might simply assign moral agency to banks (which recall Friedman refutes since he does not see 'banks' ontologically or by nature of their being as suitable candidates for agency) and then posit a set of duties which one considers appropriate. Hence, for example, one might decide banks have a duty to not lend to persons whom the bank strongly suspects will default in years to come, allowing seizure of the collateral and forfeiture of the initial deposit. Lending in this fashion was a strategy undoubtedly employed by some financial institutions before the collapse in real estate values. However, one might decide that this is not a moral activity for banks or others to pursue and include it in the list of acts from which they must refrain. It is obvious how contentious this would all become. To what extent must one's tolerance for perhaps disagreeable yet profitable practice be exercised? The extraordinary difficulty of attempting to foresee the likelihood of crises such as we have regularly experienced and eradicating activity conducive to them, via a mechanism based on an arbitrary moral framework is fraught with practical and theoretical problems. We must be wary of how *post-facto* rationalizations of events can engender false confidence as to our capacity to make *ante-facto* promulgations. Hindsight trading is not trading, in financial market-speak.

If society does decide to address issues of morality within the financial markets, (which in spite of the discomfort this seems to engender, is undoubtedly imperative), then it is likely to follow the methodology it employs in other matters of ethical concern. This tends to pit rights-based claims against those of liberty, of duties to society and interventionist attempts to alter aggregate social outcomes against the right to autonomy and a 'naturally' evolving optimality. Consider any issue affecting contemporary society with an acknowledged moral aspect and this tends to be the standard structure of the process that leads to either a consensus or a disputed but accepted conclusion. In short, a compromise.

To avoid the trap of simply politicizing these issues, I shall not suggest the format of any such framework that disputes Friedman's hypothesis and assigns social responsibilities to firms. Doubtless if any substantive change of mindset occurs with respect to the financial markets this is the road that will be travelled. One assured outcome would be increased regulation and taxation for the industry participants. Instead, in keeping with this book's aim of emphasizing the importance of philosophy to finance, I shall make a case for a rather different approach which draws heavily from the fourth main branch of ethics, namely virtue ethics. This has become deeply unfashionable, as mentioned earlier, in contemporary society. When Western politicians and commentators debate ethical matters it is almost invariably whilst standing on one of two soap-boxes; that of rights or that of consequences. The former talk of the hypothetical everyman who is born with certain rights which society is duty bound to respect, whilst the latter wish to emphasize the sum total effect that pertains to particular states of affairs, the justice of which is enough to over-ride irksome rights. Appeals to religious morality are rare and to a notion of the 'good life' rarer still. Yet I believe the ethics of the 'good life' has a contribution to make. It immediately drops the level of moral agency back down from institutions or industry to the individuals; to traders and brokers themselves. The discomfort this affords the participants and indeed the politicians, is only too obvious. But that is no reason not to proceed. And we commence not with Socrates or Aristotle or the other founders of virtue ethic philosophy, but with the man whose picture is on the dartboard of every bank chief executive: Karl Marx.

2.

There is almost nothing in Milton Friedman's ethical theory of business with which Karl Marx would disagree, in so far as the theory is an accurate description of the behaviour expected of workers and capital owners under free market capitalism. It is the desirability of the resultant state of affairs and its effect on the individuals concerned about which they would vehemently disagree. And whilst only a fool would fail to extol the productive capabilities of the capitalist system[33] in contrast to any other system hitherto devised by mankind, it is not with this element that Marx is concerned. Reducing the system to the level of the individual, Marx detected ubiquitous evidence of what German philosophy termed 'entfremdung'. This is, perhaps inadequately, translated as 'alienation'. The roots of the concept are found in Ludwig Feuerback's *Essence of Christianity*, but Marx saw the hypothesis as directly relevant to capitalism. His idea was that we may grant free-market thinkers such as Friedman his claim that the workers merely have duties to produce for the capitalists, whilst they in turn merely have a duty to obey the law, but what is lost in this is the effect this arrangement has on the worker himself, as a person.

The result, Marx argued, was a destructive alienation for the workers. They were alienated from the products they made, the process by which these were produced, the capital and profits that accrued and other human beings working elsewhere to produce the array of goods available in the economy. But most vitally of all, the worker was alienated or estranged from his own humanity.

It is monumental folly to dismiss the entire output of thinkers when certain of their claims are apparently contradicted by subsequent experience or new knowledge. The works of Newton are not ignored in their entirety because he was a known alchemist. That fact that centrally planned economies have generally failed dismally and repeatedly, and seem to come hand in hand with repressive or totalitarian despotic governance is true, but is no reason to dismiss all philosophical critiques of elements of capitalism; the two are not synonymous and nor is pure communism the only alternative to pure capitalism. The point here, which should not be dismissed out of hand, is that Marx is questioning the individualistic aspect to Friedman's model, which the latter was content to deal with only in a perfunctory manner.

Marx felt that the central outcome for human beings under capitalism or, if one prefers, under Adam Smith-style partitioned labour, was that they became estranged from their own humanity. What does this mean? Marx believed that there are two aspects to human life, namely our *existence* and our *essence*. We share existence with all living things but it is our essence that distinguishes us as humans or persons. This is constituted by our ability to reason, to express ourselves, to be creative and to live a good life. But for Marx, under capitalism, workers are alienated from these essential facets of human existence. When one is specific about these essences one finds they are generally actions and means of living typically occurring *outside* of work; enjoying the theatre, playing sport, learning how to knit, meeting friends, eating with family etc. This is what Marx means by alienation; when the worker clocks on, he leaves the essence of his humanity at the door.

Marx had observed similarly estranging forces in operation under religious hegemony but in that case it was God separating man from himself. Assessing this idea on its own merit and separating it from the subsequent ruinous experiments with communist economies inspired by Marxist thought is not easily achieved. Yet as soon as one reduces the financial industry to banks, hedge funds, brokerage houses and proprietary trading houses, and then again to bankers, 'hedgies', brokers and traders, one is left with people. Friedman's simplistic narrative is inadequate because it is an ethical theory devoid of humanity. The absence of complication derives from the estrangement of workers from their human essence. The contractual relationship is such that the labourers turns up for work, make profit for the employer and go home, where Friedman says they are at liberty to pursue whatsoever social objectives they choose. But the human essence of the workers is of no consequence in the context of this ethical theory of business.

To see how Marx's ideas are particular apposite in the financial markets, consider the life of a typical Wall Street or City trader. On graduation from University, he or she will enter a bank or trading firm and work exceedingly long hours under considerable pressure. Dealing rooms are fraught places where machismo and uncontrollable external factors blend with egoism and aggression. They will deal in products that it is humanly impossible to feel any affection for beyond a vague and limited intellectual curiosity. They may well adopt an entirely different persona in work; this is particularly common as many normal, everyday human personality traits are undoubtedly a hindrance to profitability. And profitability is the solitary end. Why do young bright people dedicate themselves to this existence? There are several reasons.

I)   To make enough money to be able to stop living this existence.

II) To make so much money that they are recognised within the industry and perhaps in society as having made lots of money/been successful; the one is often seen as a proxy for the other.

III) To finance a certain material lifestyle to which they have become accustomed in consequence of living this existence.

IV) Because they enjoy the existence.

All of these reduce to the same thing, (even the last), which is to make money, since I know not of any trader or banker who would continue in their job were the remuneration not several multiples of the average wage in the economy at large.

So money is the only true motivation. The CEOs of banks like to claim that money is in fact an irrelevance; it is more about the challenge, pitting oneself against the market and just being part of 'the game'. But this rings incredibly hollow from people paid tens of millions of dollars per year.

What of it, one might say? Profits honestly and hard earned[34] generate vast corporate and personal tax revenues. Society benefits enormously from this activity. There are many important points to contest here. Firstly, from a practical perspective, the only real contribution to society via taxation is made from the taxing of genuine value-adding profit. To see this, consider two banks, A and B engaged in a range of trading activities; if one of the desks in bank A makes a profit trading directly against a corresponding desk in bank B, then this is taxable. But bank B can *offset* these losses from its desk against its profits made elsewhere in the bank, which would otherwise be taxable. This negates the tax collected from the desk that made the profit in bank A. In other words, the tax paid by A is really just tax that would have been paid by B on true economic productiveness. The only genuine contribution comes not from the zero-sum activity, but from the activity which is generating real economic wealth in some way. Secondly, from a theoretical perspective, this is a consequentialist argument and runs entirely counter to Friedman's ethic to which the industry appears to subscribe. This is clearly an attempt to pick and choose the obligations or social responsibilities as they see fit. Furthermore, when brought down again to the level of the individual trader or banker, the argument sounds preposterous; anyone justifying their work by the amount of tax they pay seems to see themselves engaged in a largely altruistic pursuit. Does anyone truly work *primarily* in order to pay healthy amounts of taxation?

The reason why a justification is really required is that it is surely owed to the workers themselves. No-one should be content with a career whose central aim is accepted unconditionally and unquestioningly. The aim of financial trading is to make as much profit as possible for the sake of the capital provider. This much must surely be admitted. Embellishments such as 'to be successful' or 'to be challenged' are subsidiary to or euphemistic for the only serious goal which is maximising remuneration. Now the effects of this work ethic that pervades the industry, as pertains to society in general are one matter; banking and trade has much that is positive to offer. Claim and counter-claim in this regard are a matter for economists, finance theorists and policy makers. But what of the individuals concerned? What of their lives?

To work for twelve to twenty hours per day, staring at a screen of data, attempting to make a very fast buck, for ten to twenty years in order to become wealthy enough to no longer need to do this or any other kind of work again and yet live in comparative luxury. This is the personal mission statement of thousands of workers in the financial industry and is so far removed from the Classical notion of a life well lived as to render comparison difficult. In truth it amounts to a life at odds with almost any ethical philosophy founded on ideals of the highest good, conceived by philosophers to date. It is an absurd waste of the prime of life. The new wealth and substance created by such activity in many cases is either negligible (since so much of the trading is zero-sum) or so remote and secondary that the links are tenuous. In response to this observation (with which many traders willingly concur), one particular trader told me that nothing would please him more than to see the retail and investment banking divisions formally split universally, so that he could effectively ensure that he would just be gambling against known rival banks and hedge funds in the exotic over-the-counter derivatives that he traded; in other words, to see his trading and market extracted from the real economy and world such that it could have literally no effect on anything that might matter to anyone else. This is no different to playing poker for twelve hours per day at the same table with the same competitors for years on end; a nil-output Sisyphusean absurdity of a life.

The ancient ethicists saw humanity and a life well-lived in bolder and more ambitious terms than these. For despite protestation to the contrary it is for a want of true ambition that traders and the like devote some of their best years to such singular and lop-sided priorities. To expend vital years in the sole pursuit of wealth so as to begin to live the real life one desires from middle-age onwards is a Faustian pact. The virtuous life recommended by pre-Christian thinkers was built upon a search for magnanimity, knowledge, pleasure, happiness, love of wisdom, manners, friendship, truth, justice and courage. Its aim is to harmonise man with his own humanity; to avoid excess, estrangement and alienation. It revels in humanist delights, in culture and artistry.

3.

Alfred Whitehead claimed that the whole tradition of European philosophy constituted mere 'footnotes to Plato'. Profoundly original thought is as rare in philosophy as in other fields, if not rarer given the subject's unparalleled history. And so the claims above, for example concerning financial market activity and its frequent incongruity with virtue ethics, may also be charged with lacking novelty. But that we must at least re-consider the current approach is a matter made all the more pressing by the extraordinary changes afoot in the markets themselves. Extrapolation of recent innovations in derivatives markets forward to the next few decades would suggest that products of extreme complexity will emerge. Inter-relatedness across institutions is likely to increase. Theory and understanding will lag widespread usage. And whilst this will afford opportunities to create real wealth and enhance economic mechanisms, the potential for greater destruction will be ever-present. Nay-saying, reactionary, doom-mongering should not be dismissed out of hand in these matters;

derivatives in particular are purposely built to foster exponentially large outputs from simple, low-level inputs. Big bangs for the buck. Our ability to segregate users of these instruments to avoid a massive contamination of the entire system is likely to be minimal in reality. The prohibition of such products is likewise unworkable and probably undesirable for the lost benefits alone. Our careful and studied use of nuclear fission technology might be a helpful analogy. We do not eschew its use for fear of catastrophe but instead take extreme precautions. The unimaginable horror of a civil nuclear calamity serves as a constant restraining force. But collapsing derivatives markets, whose impact on the global economy would be comparably destructive by analogy, are subject to scant safety provision by regulators, financial institutions and other bodies. The recent crises have shown that while a rogue trader may bring down his bank, systemic damage is caused by traders from different institutions working with apparent independence of thought and action, but co-variantly from a macroscopic viewpoint. Complacency is not a sensible option.

That the pursuit of money in and by itself is a vacuous existence is not a new claim but one that bears repeating. Once within the walls of a dealing room, profits can have a narcotic effect. The atmosphere and décor of the trading floors are fiercely de-humanising, aiming to eliminate the need to emote, lest that should come at the expense of rational thought. Proprietary firms and hedge funds tend to favour less austere surroundings, but that the crisis scathed them less than the banks one doubts is explicable by this fact alone.

To become overly conspiratorial about the situation is to borrow too heavily from Marx. Are bankers oppressed by their capital-owning employers, sowing the seeds of their own augmented future oppression with every profitable trade they make? Can one be oppressed whilst earning $1 million dollars per annum? The answer to this question may be tied to the reason as to why banks and traders are paid such disproportionately large amounts. Indeed, they have stressful jobs, but so too do school teachers and ambulance drivers. They can be vastly profitable in a competitive environment, but this is also true of other industries where profit per employee is comparable, but remuneration is far lower. A substantial but overlooked factor in the elevated pay of bankers and traders is the difficulty in convincing tired, stressed, young and already relatively wealthy individuals to continue to give-up the overwhelming majority of their current life to work with products they cannot have any affection for, in constricted and de-humanised conditions, expressing next-to-nothing of their creative essence, for a purpose devoid of meaning to themselves and of questionable benefit (or possible detriment) to society at large. I recall a trader once asking in a dealing room how much money the others present would require to be imprisoned for ten years. One dryly replied that he knew the answer precisely. And with that, he held up his pay slip.

That there are evidently more worthy ways to live life, one doubts to be news to many traders or bankers engaged in pure speculation in esoteric and disconnected instruments. But there is much to condition them against sentiments prevailing upon them to leave; the pay, a vague sense that the financial markets are probably a good thing in general, the supposed intellectual challenge etc. And banality is hardly a feature exclusive to this form of employment; there are many pointless jobs to choose from. But for an ambitious young person of sound education and intellect, zero-sum trading is an entirely ridiculous occupation.

The swiftly evolving financial environment and the anaesthetizing effect of being fully enveloped by the system, makes the ideals of virtue ethicists worthy of promotion. And it is certainly not to propose that all bankers and traders ought to leave the industry tomorrow for a perceived worthier existence, which is a generalisation too far. Rather it is to suggest that individuals reflect on their own working life in relation to some notion of the *summum bonum*.

But can a stronger claim be made to the effect that this moral philosophy or that ethical theory is in fact *compelling?* Perhaps one has reason to be considerably more evangelical on the matter such that a polite recommendation really will not suffice? How should we react to the recalcitrant hedge fund manager who effectively speculates all day, every day, but rather takes pleasure from so doing and enjoys his lot?

Here we face running the gauntlet between absolutism and relativism. If we press very hard and insist that our notion of the good, moral life is a matter of certainty, we really ought to have a convincing proof as to why this is so. And whilst many philosophers have proclaimed an ethical theory that is supposedly logically derived from a rational metaphysic, none has persuaded humankind *as a whole* to date. Descartes, Spinoza and Kant all boasted 'compelling' theories of ethics. Plato's Socractic dialogues seem to lead 'logically' to ethical conclusions, but the premises are disputable and cannot be held as self-evident truths, which rather tarnishes the argument. But if any absolute claim that an ethical theory is correct is unattainable, does ethical theory simply dissolve into a relativist soup? The British moral philosopher Bernard Williams felt not; known for his effective dismantling of several moral philosophies ending in –ism, he still could not resign himself to a full acceptance of relativism, preferring instead scepticism and honesty. David Hume thought morality to be a function of the passions, which fact rendered impossible a conclusion arrived at by dint of pure reason. He greatly admired the ethical thinkers of antiquity but roundly disapproved of the notion that an objective foundation could be laid in consequence of which normative claims could be declared incontestable. Sentiments of disapproval regarding certain behaviour do not emanate from the behaviour itself nor from an abstract truth regarding moral action. Instead, Hume believed 'it lies in yourself, not in the object. So that when you pronounce any action or character to be vicious, you mean nothing, but that from the constitution of your nature you have a feeling or sentiment of blame from the contemplation of it'.[35] This is often termed *moral subjectivism*. The justification for an ethical judgement or theory is not rational deduction but emotional reaction. Perhaps Hume's lasting popularity as a philosopher is in part due to his brilliant exposition of ideas that chime elegantly with our natural intuition or perhaps even common-sense. In this particular case, he offers a way out of our current dilemma. Rather than claim moral authority because we believe to have an insight into some objective truth or to admit despairingly that no moral code has any formal validity or grounds compelling its adoption, we might hold that our particular ethical view carries weight because we truly *feel* it to do so. To the obvious objection that this merely reduces to matters of opinion, Hume pointed sanguinely to humanity's general benevolence and the widespread concurrence on many or most moral issues. Murder is wrong because we all feel that this is the case and for no other or better reason than this.

Whether or not this is convincing, it offers one explanation as to why there is so much overlap in disparate ethical theories throughout time and in various places, in so far as they may simply reflect human nature rather than intangible truths. And finally, as the financial crisis is analyzed and changes are made, my intention here has been to promote the claim that virtue ethics stake to be included in the political calculus. The moral subsumption of individual human beings into a business class or financial sector has the effect of extensively estranging them from much of their nature. Responsibilities or duties have nowhere to fall by designation of this system. Consequentialism has great difficulty both assigning agency and separating out the very consequences by which it means to judge. But if we attempt to root the moral sense of financial markets in the individual participants themselves, by due consideration of the *summum bonum*, we may find the consequences for society and the apparent dutifulness of financial institutions, happily take care of themselves.

4.

Thus far, our discussion of morality and the financial markets has remained largely meta-ethical. Its focus has been on the different types of ethical theories and how they may have relevance for the problems we face. It has been argued that to date, where the debate has any recognisable formal element at all, it has generally been centred on consequentialism and the morality of rights and duties. This quickly leads to difficulties when it is unclear what the direct consequences of particular actions happen to be. Knowing that banks aggregated, re-packaged and re-traded bundles of mortgages does not make it a simple affair to create a causal chain that leads directly to the financial disaster that ensued. Matters in practice can be rather more complex than the theoretical consequentialist may care to admit. What is more, the concept of causality is philosophically problematic; asserting that something or someone uniquely and unambiguously caused something can often attract controversy, in the sense that it demands a full explication of what is meant by 'to cause'. And pragmatically, there can be many obstacles; in what sense is any one specific bank culpable for the crisis, when other banks acted identically and the crisis may only have been the result of this combined behaviour? Or perhaps the bank's own behaviour was insufficient in itself to cause the crisis and had it acted otherwise the upshot would have been little different? In what manner then can we find the bank worthy of blame? In short, ethical prescriptions based on consequences at a macro-level, face great challenges that demand a very clear account as to the causal mechanisms presumed to be at work.

The other ethical mindset vaguely adopted is to suppose that financial institutions have duties resting on them which derive, presumably, from a set of rights attributable to the rest of society. So for example, one might argue that taxpayers have a right not to be leaned upon as a free put option by banks; in other words banks have a duty not to abuse the taxpayer's inability to allow the banks to collectively fail, by leveraging themselves ruinously in the knowledge that they will profit if things go their way, and be bailed out, if they do not. Several problems frequently arise with such a proposition. Firstly, the rights or duties must be elucidated with great clarity, but even then it can be doubtful to what extent they have been breached, abused or disregarded; again, matters in reality can be highly complicated. Secondly, defining the agents involved with accuracy and sound justification is made harder by the nature of the entities involved. Assigning agency to societal groupings rather than merely to individuals can be a fraught business. Finally, any right or duty proposed ought to have its existence justified. The spectre of so-called 'rights inflation' looms as ever, as too does that of rights confliction. Banks may posit a right to trade freely and legally without having to account for socialist planning (*cf* Friedman). The reality will be a fudge of some sort, if any consensus is to be reached.

The admittedly idealistic hope expressed here in the light of these problems is that whilst rights and consequences will undoubtedly form the basis of any political settlement, there remains a role for the ethics of virtue. But in the very least, the debate needs to be re-cast in far more rigorous terms than has hitherto been the case. The obvious discomfort of politicians and the ulterior and vested motives of all those in power (if not necessarily in government) are no help in this end. A pre-condition for clarity, is honesty.

So how might these ideas be useful in practical terms? Once we step down from loftier metaphysical contemplation of various ethical systems, we move closer to the real action. This field is often referred to as applied ethics. By asserting certain facts about situations, such as whom is involved in what action, and of what the likely outcomes consist, we set the scene for an ethical discussion which aims to reach a substantive judgement. This might involve judging the morality of an action or of an agent. Or it may be that an ethical verdict is deemed unattainable. Perhaps after consideration there will be an acknowledgement that, *a priori*, it is not possible to determine a morally right course of action and that therefore the agent is absolved of future blameworthiness. It is just such methods that are routinely applied by ethics committees, judges and perhaps even parents when situations arise that seem to require their due moral consideration.

Until now in this discussion of ethics, financial markets and financiers have been treated as though homogenous. This seems to have also been the accepted premise belying society's reaction to the crisis. Bankers and hedge fund traders have been tarred with identical brushes. Yet this is clearly a dangerously inadequate characterization. In part it stems from an understandable need to simplify what are extraordinarily complex states of affairs, in a world unfamiliar to most. And it would seem politicians believe it to serve them well to have a readily identifiable set of attention-deflecting baddies. The time must come however when this erroneous approximation of an assumption is removed; we must seek finer distinctions within the financial markets between institutions, functions, concepts and persons.

It would be highly ignorant to amend regulation, to admonish or to victimise before due recognition is given to the heterogeneity of financial markets, which is perhaps their most salient feature. That the metaphysical essence of banks, securities and financial concepts are so ill-understood provides no excuse for a reluctance to note the glaringly obvious diversity that the industry exhibits. An insurer insures, a pharmaceutical firm researches and devises drugs, but a bank might conduct a massively disparate number of operations. With this in mind, it is preferable to focus on actions rather than entities. This is another good reason to consider being guided by the ethics of virtue, since it pertains to individuals primarily. If agency is persistently focussed on banks as a whole, it is hard to see how virtue ethics could play a role of any significance.

Consider then some, rather than all, of the activities in which traders and bankers engage. A typical market in an instrument or financial product will consist in some or all of the following: end users (for example investors, speculators, companies looking to hedge exposure), brokers (agents between buyers and sellers), analysts (who research and make recommendations) and market makers (who provide a constant pool of liquidity). A straightforward compartmentalisation along such lines might be helpful to an ethicist looking to apportion moral agency or consider the conduct of certain participants from a moral aspect. But the tendency for those external to the industry in recent times has been to ignore any such distinctions and posit universal blame and collective responsibility. The reaction from within the industry has been to claim individual innocence; the market maker is simply providing liquidity, the analyst merely offering an opinion, the speculator just one of many and individually insignificant and so on and so forth. Perhaps this is all true and the entire crisis was the fault of nobody; it just happened to occur?

Another approach however is to look more closely at these apparently different roles and to see how clearly distinct they are. If their separation is perfect, moral agency may be more clearly allocated. The ontology of the players however is not as simple as it might appear. Traditionally, the broker and trader are thought to have very different jobs; but of course they will often function collaboratively for trading to occur. The flow is bi-directional as the brokers and analysts may recommend trades to the speculator or investor, whilst the latter furnishes the broker with information concerning the market which will often be recycled and integrated into recommendation and comment made to other clients. The extent to which this activity is truly separable is probably limited. Likewise the market maker, who traditionally or hypothetically, takes no *directional* view on the market (unlike the investor or speculator) but tries to minimise his exposure by very frequent buying and selling. However in reality it becomes all but inevitable that he adopts a speculative stance of one sort or another. The moment that he acquires inventory of any description, he must begin to have care for the likely direction of the market. If end users have a collective bias regarding the direction of any instrument's price, the market maker, (who is notionally neutral in that he aims to off-set all his trades between *disagreeing* end users) will be prone to be non-neutral. In this instance, (which is common), is the market maker not now speculating by default? When end-users trade in order to hedge away their exposure, it is natural to suppose this is *anti-speculative* behaviour. After all, they are reducing rather than increasing their risk, possibly to nothing. When for example an airline company knows it must buy aviation fuel in six month's time, it would seem at first glance that by trading in the appropriately specified futures or forward contract they can reduce the risk of a sharp rise in fuel prices between now and when purchase of the fuel is unavoidable. This activity seems entirely different from that typically thought speculative. And yet, on closer inspection, and as any hedger will report by virtue of experience, no such hedge is entered into without a consideration as to the possible future moves of prices in the market concerned. Although hedging can reduce exposure almost to zero, the decision as to whether to hedge or not, requires an estimation of the likely intervening price movements. The decision to trade therefore (i.e. to execute the hedge position) is contingent on one's disposition to the future price moves, but this is also the essence of *speculative* activity. This is a typically paradoxical result of philosophical reasoning. Whilst hedging and speculation appear contrary, in a most crucial regard, they are indistinct.

So whilst the various traditional roles that market participants fulfil are distinct in theory (and in much of the academic financial literature) the reality for those participants will be more opaque. This means that whilst it is not appropriate to tar entire markets or industries with the same brush, in many cases the professed inculpability of some participants when things as a whole go awry in a market demands careful scrutiny. I am yet to meet any dealer in sub-prime, collateralized debt or credit default swaps who admits to a conscience that is anything but clear, and often this plea of innocence is accompanied with an uncharacteristic self-effacement; "Ah, but I was only a broker" for example. My point here is not to dismiss such claims out of hand but to suggest rather that the functions that people in the markets assume are not, *per se*, so inseparable as to preclude them from blame when it is apportioned by function *simpliciter*. In other words, if speculators were deemed the villains of the piece, the rest of the market may not necessarily evade admonishment legitimately by claiming full non-speculator status. There may be a very real sense in which they are indeed all in unwitting cahoots.

So, simple distinctions drawn along the line of job descriptions may prove fallible. Another approach is to look at specific action and its motivation. The market maker may accept that his role has a speculative element but that the greater part of his occupation is to help the market function efficiently. And this may be a rather good thing, with the fruits of capitalist production brought more easily to bear. But the speculator's role may need stiffer reinforcement if another distinction is admitted; namely that between an investor and a speculator.

The question of how and if speculation differs from investment is central to much of the applied ethics of financial markets. The two seem to connote quite different activities, but more from cultural inheritance than obvious analytic distinction. The speculator has a strong association with the gambler, which has always been attended to with moral indignation in certain quarters. He takes risks for the sake of profit alone. The investor on the other hand seems to have a more virtuous reputation. There appears an inherent notion that he is giving of himself in some way; putting something in. He too seeks a return like the speculator and is a risk-taker, but he acts boldly rather than recklessly and contributes to society by engendering growth of some kind.

In a great many cases this supposed obvious distinction is utter nonsense. The overwhelming majority of 'investors' in financial markets are disinterested, inactive owners of securities, held and traded via agents with little or no precise knowledge as to the detail. Pension funds hold massive inventory in stocks and bonds on behalf of such 'investors' who often have little awareness of the content of their portfolios. Their money is at risk and their chief concern is that the prices of their assets should rise. It is hard to disassociate this with very basic speculation.

Once again, care must be taken. We ought not to look to demonise a certain function such as speculation unless we have a very thorough understanding of the term. But time and again we hear loose talk from politicians, commentators or even central bankers bemoaning casino-like activity in the markets or base speculation. Unfortunately, things are neither so simple nor well enough understood as to permit blanket condemnations of this sort.

It would be a great pity if the analysis thus far has served to make the application of ethical philosophy to financial markets appear a particularly difficult endeavour. In response to this, it ought to be noted that a task being problematic is rarely a sufficient reason in itself to not attempt an undertaking. Furthermore, ethical problems elsewhere are often complex and inscrutable, being as they are a function of human interaction and conceptual issues. Finally, there are some instances where perhaps things are a little more clear-cut. For example, a recent fashion has been to include raw commodities in the set of all assets or investment opportunities. This trend has coincided with a strong bull market in the price of many such natural resources, from agricultural produce to precious and industrial metals to livestock. Now a case is made that these increases in prices are caused by the increased productive and consumptive habits of developing nations. Simple arguments that if industrial growth exceeds productivity gains in mining, extracting and refining, then the upward shift in the demand function cannot be met by supply and prices must rise. Rapid population expansion in developing economies, accompanied by economic growth, increases the domestic propensity to consume manufactured goods and more diverse foodstuffs. The marginal improvement in basic resource harvesting is limited by the logical notion that the lowest hanging fruit has already been picked for the more developed world's consumption. Such is one narrative of the 'commodity story'. Increasing demand and restricted supply will ensure rising prices in the future.

Now whilst this is far from guaranteed, it has an initial plausibility. Whether and to what extent this projection is factored into *current* prices is perhaps unknowable. But if one agrees with the sentiment, then apportioning some greater of lesser part of one's wealth to the purchase of such raw materials may appeal. This is now, (unlike in even the recent past), a possibility for the man on the street through the use of structured products, exchange traded funds or other pseudo-derivative contracts. He has the means to gain exposure to these goods, if not via direct purchase and sale, then by a contract with a counterparty (typically an investment bank) who will in turn replicate the coverage he seeks. By this method, anyone with even modest wealth may synthetically expose it to the price movements of crude oil, cattle, soybeans, platinum or some combination of such commodities.

But the inclusion of commodities into the class of all assets is not uncontroversial. There is dispute as to what constitutes a true asset and a commonly denoted necessary feature is the yielding of a return or dividend. A bond for example may pay its owner a coupon; a certificate of deposit, an interest rate. A company is owned for the profit is produces. But commodities are zero-yielding. Indeed, they are more keenly associated with cost of carry (storage costs) such that they are often negatively-yielding. Aside from the earlier caveat that certain 'assets' yield nothing for their owner (such as zero coupon bonds), there is a school of thought that feels happier considering commodities not so much as assets but more as stores of wealth, a proxy for money or simply as objects, the price of which may be speculated upon.

The distinction between investment and speculation is, as discussed, not as clear as is sometimes thought. Perhaps in this case however, we can be more confident in our appraisal. In so far as commodities are not held in a portfolio with the view to mitigate the effects of raw material inflation, it might be argued that their acquisition in the hope of price rises *alone* is purely speculative. There is no sense in which the holder sees this deployment of capital as a source of economic enhancement or growth in itself, such as in the case of a corporate bondholder. This is obviously true since the commodity is inert; a lump of gold has no capacity to grow at all, let alone of its own accord. Indeed, the holder of commodities, in simply hoping to see prices rise as the sole ends to his ownership, would probably welcome a *decline* in the productive capacity or efficacy of miners or farmers. General economic growth he may welcome, in as much as this is commensurate with increased demand and prices, for his holding. But an augmentation of human productive capabilities with respect to his holdings specifically, is against his interest.

I think this an instance where the morality of a certain practice in the free and fair financial markets is certainly questionable and under circumstances where the *economic* case may be highly compelling for the holder himself. To see this, let us assume that the buyer is convinced by the commodity story and believes firmly that prices will rise. He sees this as a threat to the future purchasing power of his personal wealth, as future purchases he will make, for which he would like to set aside some money now, will cost more due to the increase in raw material prices. But furthermore he perceives in this an opportunity for profit. If he hedges the inflationary threat by buying some commodities in some proportion estimated to eliminate the corrosive impact on his purchasing power, then acquisition over and beyond this amount is intended to increase his wealth disproportionately. In what sense is this morally problematic? Surely this is simply capitalism at work; he is just re-allocating resources, which is very much the essence of capitalism.

Well, perhaps on one reading. But consider this situation less solipsistically for a moment. The holder of the commodity aims to profit from the need of others to use the commodity for consumption or production. In particular, he estimates that those in the developing world will increasingly demand the commodity. It is hard therefore not to see the trade as mere hoarding to profit from and indeed to encourage higher prices. Not only this, but it is hoped that poorer nations will be the ones to fuel the demand. So in effect an 'investor' in the developed world who has excess wealth for his current needs is devoting this surplus to ensuring the supply of natural resources is restricted. Now if capitalism simply involves free and open movements of capital, then there seems little to add here by way of comment. But if capitalism is thought to be more a setting for entrepreneurialism, then this is a stiffer test for the commodity hoarder to pass. If we accept the idea of economist J-B Say that entrepreneurialism is the pro-active business of re-allocating resources from low to high yielding prospective ventures, (which by definition enhances overall prosperity) then there seems little entrepreneurially praise-worthy about the commodity buyer's action. Indeed by ensuring the materials are put to no productive use whatsoever, he acts as an anti-entrepreneur. And as stated, he has a disposition to see productivity more widely fall.

Judged by an ethical code based upon consequentialism, it is impossible to condone these actions. The commodity hoarder stands to benefit in measure precisely matched by the infelicity of others, and there is a likelihood and expectation that these others will be of poorer stock than the hoarder. The *aggregate* outcome summates to zero, but an alternative, counterfactual, more prosperous state of affairs was available, had the hoarder's initial excess capital been put to productive use. Its allocation to scarce resources will immediately increase their prices, to the detriment of all users thereof. The world is certainly not a happier place, in sum, for these actions.

Do the ethics of duties or rights offer anything besides stricture to the hoarder? This really does depend upon which set of rights or duties one wishes to see universally acknowledged. If one sees as inviolable the right of the hoarder to park his capital wheresoever he sees fit subject to law, then one may as well abandon any ethical consideration under this reading of capitalism. To appeal to a sense that morality is irrelevant is effectively just to employ ammoralism. Whilst a consistent and valid view, do not the string of financial crises experienced in the last 80 years suggest its inadequacy? To reach a moral verdict of sorts with respect to the actions of the commodity stock-piler, we must posit a conflicting and inviolable right of the dispossessed to not be exploited whilst assigning a duty to respect this said right by the resource owner. And here we descend once again into murky metaphysical waters as to whose rights trump whose. This would seem a matter of subjective preference at heart and so the relatively clear assessment of the consequentialist or utilitarian ethicist is unlikely to be matched by the deontologist.

Excluding again any Christian view on the situation (which with regards to the literal accumulation of worldly goods is surely so obvious as to need no further comment), we come to virtue ethics. Once again we ought to stress that not all moral philosophies founded on notions of the *summum bonum* concur with one another, nor are any accepted as infallibly justified or objectively true. Perhaps the highest good and measure of a life well lived is thought to consist in the appropriation of the greatest portion of physical goods and to strive to be the richest man in the graveyard? I have no doubt that for some this is indeed a living creed; and in the financial markets more commonly than elsewhere. If this is held to the case then there is very little one can say to the contrary such as to deduce a contradiction. I am unaware of any formal unarguable proof that this belief is objectively and plainly misguided. But a sorry life is this if it is true.

Of the many activities in which bankers, traders and financiers engage, some will offer greater opportunity than others for us to say with confidence that their existence is either welcome or unseemly. A total exoneration of commercial activity from ethical consideration beyond very basic rules of conduct may provide an easy and consistent framework but its simplicity or shallowness is unlikely to satisfy complex societal needs, as recent experience suggests. We are happy in other walks of life to reach ethical judgements, imperfect as we recognise them to be, without despairing as to the difficulty of the task or resorting to ammoralism cloaked by a supposed liberalism. The alienation or estrangement that capitalism does to some extant entail, has a compounding effect that is most unwelcome in this regard and against which the methods of moral philosophy can preserve our vigilance.

Chapter 7

1.

Robert thumped the desk with his fist, breaking the silence and startling the others in the dealing room.

"This fucking guy!" he shouted.

No-one said anything in reply. Robert traded in an illiquid and esoteric European derivatives market. The products involved were used by a handful of professionals and a small batch of end-users. But by and large the trading that did occur was to and fro between a select group of institutional traders that included Robert; a bridge table might have more players than this particular market on some days. There was one competitor in particular however who concerned Robert. Time and again, whoever he was, he seemed to be jamming the market against Robert's position. He didn't know which firm the chap worked for, (although he had his suspicions), but he was prepared to admit that he knew how to trade. No sooner did Robert put on a trading position than the competitor was on the electronic screens, marking it heavily against him. This could last for days or even weeks until Robert was finally beaten into submission, cut his losses and closed out the position. Yet no sooner did he do this but it seemed the guy would start marking things back the other way. Had Robert just held on, he would have made back the losses instead of locking them in.

So often was this happening that Robert had begun to suspect even his own co-workers of leaking information about his portfolio. Perhaps his phone was tapped or someone in back office was being bribed by a competitor? These were not claims to be made lightly however and, with no obvious evidence, Robert preferred to take out his frustration on his desk and his brokers. He abused the brokers all day long, accusing them of lying and betraying him; he knew they would still call him for prices no matter how wildly and inaccurately he accused them. That's what brokers did.

Finally he admitted defeat. He could not bear to watch the on-screen market any longer; everyday was like a ten hour car crash, with Robert at the wheel. He decided to move into a much more liquid market where no single player could dominate the proceedings or dictate matters simply because he had deeper pockets.

So Robert closed out his position and started to trade in one of the benchmark European derivatives markets, with huge flow and daily turnover. But a week later, Robert was clearly no happier. One of the nearby traders turned to him and asked what was bothering him. Robert turned away from the screen.

"I can't believe it. This fucking guy. He's in this market too."

2.

Epistemology is the study of the theory of knowledge. It deals with questions such as what constitutes knowledge, how it is attained and to what extent is its acquisition limited? Its relevance to finance should be self-evident, this being a knowledge-based industry. When banks act in an advisory capacity, they are selling knowledge directly. When hedge funds speculate on sector swaps they are trading on their conviction that they have superior knowledge to the rest of the market. Stipulations regarding the disclosure of pertinent information by publicly floated companies are carefully designed to ensure knowledge is available in a seemly and fair manner. 'Insider trading' is a matter of considerable ethical and legal relevance, but is very much an epistemological issue. It involves attempting to categorize certain types of knowledge, assessing how it is attainable and forming normative judgements.

The study of knowledge is one of the major branches of the philosophic tradition. As ever, it is not wholly separable from other fields of enquiry; whether objective truth is knowable or exists is a metaphysical question as well as epistemic. The extent to which knowledge gleaned by induction is indeed knowledge is a matter of logic and the philosophy of scientific method. The impact of knowledge or more precisely its conference on an individual or group, as pertains to moral responsibility or duty is an ethical and epistemic philosophical issue. To what degree does the order of separation between a savvy banker trading sub-prime mortgage bundles and the naïve, defaulting sub-prime borrower matter in view of the knowledge that each may be thought to have? To what extent is it incumbent on any lender to anticipate and apprehend the true knowledge that the borrower themselves has of their own situation and the contract into which they are entering? Can a lender reasonably be expected to ever have full insight of this sort, and, if not, does this provide a cogent mitigation for when a crisis in the credit market occurs?

Such examples of epistemic questions reveal that knowledge lies at the crux of financial markets. Yet little academic or commercial consideration seems to have been given to the philosophical view of knowledge in this particular field. This is a great pity, since this is one of the deepest wells in philosophy from which to draw water. Questions regarding knowledge in a general sense have been considered from the earliest occasions. But once again we find the industry and society happy to accept as given and self-evident the most elemental concepts and objects upon which everything substantial rests. Assumptions go unquestioned, predictions prove awry, markets 'misbehave', models are altered at the margins and the next crisis is propagated. At what point will an enlightened approach be taken that does not accept anything as given?

Robert (who left the industry within weeks) was epistemologically unaware. His mistake was to reach an erroneous conclusion as to the state of affairs in his world but furthermore to fail to realise the fallibility of his capacity to acquire knowledge. His beliefs about knowledge were faulty, yet he repeatedly predicated his actions upon them. A different, more philosophical, approach was required.

3.

To consider Robert's predicament and subsequent error in a more formal way, it is necessary to suggest some initial categorisations. These will be made up of the various *types* of knowledge and again by the various means of *acquiring* knowledge. That there are different types of knowledge is recognised in say the French and German verbs translated dually in English by 'to know' (savoir/connaitre, wissen/kennen). This splitting reflects the intuitive difference between knowledge of an acquaintance variety and that of a fact or proposition. Robert may know London, he may know how to sing in tune and he may 'know' that 'this guy' is continually getting one over on him. These are all different types of knowledge, respectively; of acquaintance, of capacity or ability and of propositions. It is the latter with which we are here most concerned.

Propositional knowledge is that which is concerned with the state of affairs. Any fact about the world, the activity in a market, the weather, my height relative to yours, is propositional. So we are interested in what it means to claim to know such things and by what method(s) we can reliably come by this knowledge.

It transpires that defining knowledge is no simple task. And by a definition is meant a philosophical analysis of the concept of knowledge which typically generates necessary and sufficient conditions such that potential knowledge might be suitably classified. Common-sense or intuitive characterisation of knowledge might be thought in advance perfectly adequate to such an end, but fuller consideration shows them to be otherwise. Most ordinary attempts to explain knowledge fail to separate that which is true and good from that which is erroneous. There will be things that one thinks one knows which are not in point of fact true. But how should one make this distinction and why does it matter? The standard starting place in looking to giving meaning to knowledge is to suggest that it is a belief in a true proposition and that holding the belief is justifiable. This definition is known to be insufficient, but for now let us take its terms in sequence and see how Robert could have benefited from appreciating its sentiment.

Knowledge is a belief. This seems plausible in that if I claim to know something, I seem to hold it mentally to be the case. I am disposed to think that this something is really true, and this sounds very much like a belief. Could the opposite hold? In other words could knowledge not be a belief but something else? It is hard to see how this could be the case. If we consider our mental faculties including a collection of facts in whose veracity we have utmost confidence, it seems rather hard to argue that these do not constitute beliefs. "I don't believe this to be true, I know it!" is surely not meant literally with the implication that knowledge in some way *precludes* belief. If one knows something, one must also believe in it, making the knowledge therefore a certain type of belief.

Knowledge is a belief *in a true proposition*. This can catch people out. If we believe something to be the case, this should only be 'upgraded' to knowledge if the something is indeed the case. If John believes ours is one of many Universes, this is something he can *know* only if it is indeed true. Else it is just a belief in an untrue proposition and that is surely not knowledge. This condition can be unsettling since it creates a test for knowledge which presumably we already think our belief has passed, else we would cease to hold the belief. If John believes in God's existence, to count this belief as knowledge requires God to exist. But given that John already believes this to be the case, it suggests he has already given the matter some consideration and it is this circularity that is disquieting. And what of belief in propositions that are true but only coincidentally so? If John believes he sees Paul in the bar but is mistaken and yet Paul is indeed in the bar but out of John's line of sight, John has a belief in a true proposition but surely this fluke cannot be knowledge? To this end is added the third necessary condition that the belief must be justified. So John's seeing someone whom he mistook for Paul is not a sound justification for believing, and therefore knowing, that Paul is in the pub. To claim knowledge then requires a valid and relevant justification.

Together these conditions form jointly necessary criteria that characterise knowledge. Sadly this model is not without detractors and there are indeed counter-examples discrediting it to an extent. However it marks a very useful starting point to begin epistemological discussions and many of the attempts to eliminate the defects involve the addition of extra criteria to exclude the awkward exceptions. And it certainly still has insight to offer the hapless ex-trader Robert.

Recall that he thought he knew that one particular trader elsewhere was actively working against him. When Robert bought something, this Scarlet Pimpernel of the markets appeared and sold everything in sight, causing prices to drop precipitously. When Robert sold or went short, his nemesis went on a buying spree causing prices to leap higher and Robert would once again be left reeling. There is no doubt that Robert believed this version of events to be the case; he believed it to the extent that he eventually exited that particular market, proving it was a belief he held very firmly. But was this belief justified? We may say that it was not perhaps wholly without justification. The hypothesis did offer an explanation of the data. It also seemed to make accurate forecasts as to what would happen if Robert traded one way or another. However, it was only one of many such stories that could also fully account for the observations. That it was a simple explanation did not make the justification any stronger. And the empirical basis from which the conclusion was drawn was, as shall be discussed later, exceedingly narrow. But nevertheless there was arguably some form of justification belying his belief.

So Robert believed, and had a justification of sorts for so doing, that he knew what was going on. Was this genuine knowledge? We can say with near certainty that it was not, since the underlying proposition, 'This one guy is killing my position, all day, every day in both markets in which I have traded' was a falsehood. In the illiquid market, the possibility of one player 'bullying' the others is real although probably rare. But in the massively liquid and active market into which Robert then moved, there is virtually no realistic possibility that the proposition could still be true. Robert's 'knowledge' of the state of affairs, was no such thing, on this reading.

Whilst conceding that our analysis of knowledge is far from complete, it is still worthwhile considering how this can be applied more extensively in the financial markets. As the crisis played out through 2008 the accusation was often levelled that bankers and regulators should have known what was occurring and acted in a more pre-emptive capacity. Translated into the formal language of the analysis of knowledge, they should have formed beliefs with firm justifications that were reflective of the true state of the world and acted appropriately thereafter. Is this criticism fair? Well, a condition to this objection being sustained is that such knowledge is attainable. Some critics seem to go further however and declare that it would have been impossible for those involved to be ignorant i.e. to have no knowledge of the occurring disaster. The truth of the proposition that a financial crisis was emerging in 2008, in hindsight, seems indubitable. This leaves us then questioning whether beliefs could justifiably have been formed by the relevant parties or, *a fortiori*, if in fact they could not reasonably have been avoided. And to answer this, we must consider how it is that we come to acquire knowledge.

4.

Smith is daydreaming, thinking to himself. He has a nagging feeling that he has forgotten something. Noticing his calendar on the wall, he sees a circled date. He recognises it as the day after tomorrow and recalls marking it to remind him of Jones' birthday. He remembered the date as three months exactly after his brother's birthday. To be sure, he calls Jones' wife, who confirms the date. He tells himself that he must remember to get a card on the way home.

In this innocuous incident, Smith used all the principle methods available to us to acquire knowledge. *Perception* is the acquisition of data by our senses; taste, touch, smell, sight and sound. Smith saw the circled date and heard the testimony of Jones' wife. *Reasoning* can give grounds for belief and in turn knowledge; here Smith had a rational function that took him from a date he could confidently recall (his brother's birthday) to a date he was apt to forget. *Memory* is another source of data. Smith recalled circling the date for a specific purpose. Intuition, subliminal or sub-conscious thoughts or vague nagging feelings form a hazier category but are also generally accepted as grounds for belief of some sort. Finally Smith thought to himself or *introspected*; he was self-aware and brought the propositional fact of Jones' imminent birthday to his own attention. This is also considered a source of belief.

This list is far from exhaustive but if one considers something that one owns to be knowledge, its source is likely to be found in some or all of these modes of acquisition. So to what extent are these faculties available to financial market participants and observers such that they may acquire true justified beliefs or knowledge? On close inspection their availability is surprisingly limited for a so-called knowledge industry.

Perception, or the use of the senses, is decidedly our most productive source of empirical data. Despite claims by 17th century rationalists that true knowledge emerges via reason alone, a less extreme position surely accepts our sensory experience of the world around us to be of genuine value in the pursuit of knowledge. But for bankers, traders and financiers, the intangible essence of that in which they deal, handicaps them at a stroke as regards perception. This observation can be dismissed by those within the markets all too readily. That derivatives cannot be physically touched, or that the corporate financier cannot smell the bond issuance he is arranging is not entirely inconsequential. The fact that a corporate bond has no property relevant to sensory perception might be thought to entail that the non-applicability of one or more of our senses, comes at no cost. But regardless of this, it remains that what can be known about these products will often be inaccessible to our perceptive faculties. When contrasted to products of a tangible nature, some enviable differences are apparent. A tool manufacturer may build a physical prototype of a product; he may test the product and see the results for himself. He may see or hear outcomes that he had failed to predict in advance by use of reasoning alone. If sensory perception offered no distinct expedience to the tool manufacturer in this regard, or if forethought alone would yield no lesser amount of knowledge as to the product's efficacy and worth, then no physical prototype would ever be constructed. Intangibility is dismissed as an irrelevance when it is perhaps the most striking feature of the entire suite of financial products.

Perception is not completely unavailable of course. Financiers can hear the opinions of their customers and colleagues. They can read written accounts. But these sources are secondary to a greater or lesser extent. The question then remains as to how the people providing this information came by it; agency has simply been shifted. Perception is not necessarily in this case a primary cause. Traders may run simulations in spreadsheets or set a strategy loose on the market, tracking the profits and losses analogously to the prototype builder. This would indeed seem to count as empirical data garnered by perceptive means. But as we saw in the case of luckless Robert, the limitations of this method are inherent. To a trader sitting in a remote office, in contact with the products of his business by computer terminal alone, the sensory experience is decidedly unnatural and muted. I consider the consequences of this to be profoundly important and much overlooked. But before investigating further, let us analyse the other means of acquiring knowledge the financier may employ.

We rely heavily in daily life on our memory as a source of knowledge. If we wish to know something for longer than an instant, and perhaps for all perpetuity, we must commit it to memory. And its use is in situations that confront us which are identical to or bear close resemblance to those we have encountered before. If I am asked the location of the Eiffel Tower, I may set off on a journey of indeterminate length, directing myself at random until I find the Tower. I may look up the answer online or in a reference work. Both methods use perceptively acquired evidence to generate the requisite knowledge. More conveniently, I may recall that I have memorised the information previously. This introspection leads to my memory and so to data that may correspond to the knowledge in question. In this way then memory is previously acquired knowledge that can be re-cycled or, in combination with other methods such as reasoning, lead to distinct and original knowledge.

Now bankers and traders have access to their own memories or experiences. But the limitation of their personal circumstance is only too obvious. Even the most experienced of financiers will have memories relevant to but a fraction of the markets' depth and breadth. Many markets antedate every living trader. There will be junior traders in banks today who have no direct memory of the financial crisis of 2008. Furthermore, accumulating memories is a process which cannot be accelerated. Ten full years of experience of syndicated loan activity in actuality takes no less than ten years to acquire. Accepting this reality, market participants aim to synthesize memories in some way. They attempt to tap in to the memories of others in a hypothetical manner. And so we witness a great propensity to study charts. No other industry is so wedded to historic data as a proxy for memory and experience. So keen is the belief in memory as a source of knowledge as to the market's true nature, that it is even posited that the market *itself* has memory. This is the basis of Chartism and various wave-theories and technical theories that suggest that the constituents of all markets at all times were and are ultimately people.[36] Heterogeneous as individuals but homogeneous enough on average to suggest patterns of behaviour will recur in time. An alternative reading is to see the market as almost animated in some fashion; having a life, and therefore memories, of its own. And whilst knowledge from personal memory of say how markets reacted to the credit problems of 1929 is unavailable to almost everybody, memory by proxy might be available via the history books and graphs of price data. Memory is roundly seen to be of profound importance to financial market participants as regards the creation and retention of knowledge.

The other critical source of knowledge in the financial markets is the use of reason. This takes two main forms; *a priori* thinking and *a posteriori* thinking. Traditionally, *a priori* rationalizing is thinking which occurs prior to any direct experience. A simple example might be the mathematical proposition that 2+2=4. This knowledge can be arrived at from the comfort of an armchair with no external stimulus. It is not necessary to go out into the world finding two pairs of objects which when all summed consistently yield four. 2+2=4 is true by virtue of the meaning of the symbols and no practical experimentation is required to arrive at this knowledge. In the financial markets, this form of reasoning manifests itself in the theoretical modelling techniques employed. For instance, the Black-Scholes option pricing model provides a mathematical function to value option contracts under certain hypothetical assumptions. This function is deduced as a logical consequence of the assumptions. Theoretically then, the result is perfectly valid and rests upon no empirical input but simply on the definitions of the algebraic symbols. This is *a priori* reasoning used to create knowledge.

The counterpart to *a priori* reasoning is *a posteriori*. The two differ fundamentally approximately along the lines of deductive and inductive methods. *A posteriori* thinking draws on experiences or observations which are assimilated to arrive at theories that explain the data. The knowledge that this reasoning emits relates to driving, causal mechanisms that may not have been directly observed. This contrasts with *a priori* methods which begins with an assumed mechanism and logically determines what the outcome must *necessarily* be. One might observe the share prices of retailing companies rising simultaneously and markedly. One might then suggest that this is being driven by a perceived increase in consumer confidence; shoppers with confidence might then be expected to spend more willingly, retailing companies ought to benefit and hence their share prices may rise. This is an *a posteriori* suggestion, argued by induction and use of data, as to what may be causing the observed effect and it may constitute knowledge. It argues in the light of experience rather than by dint of pure logical analysis.

Thus, we have in outline the principle methods of acquiring knowledge available to the financier in a general sense. And of course, in many cases they are just as those available to people in every situation. But from these broad categories such as perception, memory and reasoning, we can consider the specific idiosyncrasies of the financial markets and whether this has important implications for any investigation into the financial markets.

5.

With regards to the abstract notion of knowledge, in the financial markets it is striking, and perhaps counter-intuitive, that the means of acquiring knowledge are overtly limited. For all the colossal quantities of numerical data in endless real-time publication, it is impossible not to see financiers as perceptively impaired in relation to their environment. Indeed it is surely true that the voluminous statistical output results from a tacit acknowledgement of the extent of these deficiencies. To know whether propositions regarding a publicly traded company are true might necessitate a perceptive insight that is entirely unavailable. Knowledge regarding the effective functioning or otherwise of say a Brazilian production line, might well be best attained by physically visiting the plant. But for a trader who perhaps covers an entire sector of such multinational companies, the impossibility of the task is obvious. To this end, the insight due to perception that is forfeited is substituted for a proxy in the form of numerical summary. How seamlessly this substitution can be made is highly questionable. There are those in the markets who do not believe perception should be so readily discarded and in consequence there are indeed successful analysts and fund managers whose remit is a very narrow selection of companies with whom they become personally acquainted. They will visit mines, check machinery and speak to the labourers; they will visit customers of the companies to hear their testimony and likewise with suppliers. But such analysts are the exception to the rule. The finance industry believes wholeheartedly that a spreadsheet is not only a satisfactory sensory stimulus, but in fact allows for a massive increase in intellectual productivity and the discovery of knowledge. No other industry[37] has a greater conviction in the notion that numbers may be equated with knowledge.

The usefulness of memory as a font of knowledge to those in the markets is also doubtful. Notoriously, memory recall is fallible. False memories will generate false beliefs or unjustifiably held true beliefs, but certainly not knowledge. The limited rate at which memories are accrued has already been noted. I have known traders with astonishing memories, (in particular with regards to what traded when, by whom and at what price). Instant recall of such material, coupled with reasoning, can potentially offer genuine and profitable knowledge. But on the whole, personal memory is a very blunt tool with which to carve new knowledge in the financial markets. And at worst, it can generate spurious beliefs when recall is imperfect or the accompanying reasoning is faulty. A doctor may recall seeing a patient's symptoms many times before in other patients and infer that the underlying causal mechanism of the problem is the same. That the casual mechanism could be a law of nature (e.g. the consequence of a virus acting as viruses are apt to do) means that the symptoms he sees repeatedly have definite reason to be alike. But for the financier, such rules or laws are generally opaque, if they exist at all. The conclusion drawn therefore from remembered, repeated occurrence of like events is far more likely to be fallacious. Yet day in, day out, market practitioners pore over historic charts and figures, looking for patterns, the graphs acting as synthetic memories. The strength of any justification for beliefs thus established is certainly exposed to criticism.

As to reasoning, the bankers and friends face problems arising from attempts to glean knowledge from both *a priori* and *a posteriori* methods. Theoretical models generate genuine knowledge; they can do no other when rationally formulated from premises to conclusions. To believe in these models is most certainly to be knowledgeable. Understanding a theoretical pricing model of say a coupon paying bond with explicit assumptions in place is knowledge as reliable as knowing that 2+2=4. However, this certainty vanishes when the models are applied to reality. This is probably the single greatest fallacy in evidence in financial markets today. Validly constructed theoretical models are sound and true, in theory. But for belief in them to remain as knowledge when they are applied to actuality, an extra constraint must be satisfied, namely that *every* theoretical assumption made in the model's formulation will hold in reality for so long as the model is to be applied. So, if I build a pricing model for copper futures that assumes a risk-free interest rate of r, a rate of copper mining technological progress of y, and a certain politico-social framework, to generate a theoretical price p for the futures, then if my deductive steps along the way are validly made, belief in this theory is true knowledge. In practice however, if just one of these assumptions does not hold, the truth of the model cannot be guaranteed and justification for belief therein is weakened; in short, this no longer counts as knowledge. Yet time and again, banks and hedge funds bet the house that the correspondence between the hypothetical and real is sufficiently close or near perfect so as to make the knowledge genuine and profitability appear guaranteed.

The *a posteriori* situation is little better. Here we are back to the problem the markets have to contend with of induction and an absence of credibly identifiable casual machinery. If one observes some phenomenon in the market and attempts to explain this by a rule which one takes to be knowledge and upon which future behaviour can be comfortably predicted, then this action is only justifiable to the extent that the knowledge is good and proper. But the use of inductive reasoning cannot be shown to be infallible and so justification for a belief in the explanatory mechanism proposed is diminished accordingly. So true knowledge is reduced to probabilistic belief and no doubt many participants realise this to be the case. And yet the perpetual self-assuredness which many traders and bankers affect, causes one to doubt that acceptance of this fact is universal.

This leads on to a further important issue with regards to epistemological objectivity and subjectivity. If we suppose that there are objective truths, we ought to consider whether we can come to know them, impartially. This is a rather tricky technical issue so perhaps it is best expounded in the context most relevant to our discussion. If a trader has a belief that he considers to be knowledge and upon which he is content to take a material position, it is right to ask how this change in state (i.e. assuming a material position) impinges on the objectivity of his judgement thereafter. Consider a proposition from which you are personally detached in the sense that you have no particular personal interest in its truth or falsehood. Assume that you still have justification for establishing a belief concerning the proposition, for example, perhaps you have some strong sensory evidence. Maybe it is suggested to you that it is raining in Kuala Lumpur and you can gather evidence from some source or other as to the truth of this claim. But now consider that if it is raining in Kuala Lumpur, you stand to lose a great deal of money. Or that you have the opportunity to bet on such an eventuality. Maintaining complete objectivity with regards to the process of acquiring true, justified belief is no longer so simple. You have a strong desire for a certain state of affairs to be true; you *want* to believe something to be the case. You are no longer disinterested in the way the empirical data points. And it seems likely that the higher the stakes involved become, the greater the dilution of one's objectivity.

In so far as I assert this at all, I do so by inductive reasoning. It is from years of observation that I suggest that many financial market participants struggle against subjectivity in the pursuit of knowledge when they are materially affected by its discovery. Someone 'talking their book' is the phrase used to denote those whose portfolio stands to profit from the veracity of their propositional claims and it is often used in such context as to connote that those making the claims publicly, do so in order to convince themselves as much as others.

This is a very natural, human trait. Believing what one wishes to believe and desires to be true. Seeing what one would like to see. Against this clouding of judgement it is incumbent on traders, bankers and even politicians to fight. Not wanting to believe something is happening, will not mean that it will not. When Governments happily collected massive tax revenues from the apparent profits of the financial sector in the years prior to 2008, it was understandable that they had no desire to probe too deeply into how such profits were actually being generated. They wanted all to be well, since it suited *their* 'book' for it to be so. In this sense, they were no less guilty of wilful ignorance than the bankers who had lent so ruinously. Those who assert that bankers and regulators must have seen the storm clouds gathering and should have acted to mitigate the effects, ignore the important degree of reflexivity that exists between belief, profits and desire, as distinct from truth itself. Doubtless the precariousness of the system was entirely apparent to many of those involved. And a strong-minded few maintained an emotional stoicism that preserved their objectivity of thought. Note that this did not necessarily mean they betted against the bubbles; many *knew* bubbles were forming and decided it was less risky to go with the flow rather than against it. But the enormity of the potential catastrophe for many was probably reason enough not to dwell too hard upon its likelihood. Far simpler to cross the fingers and focus on research, comment and opinion that reinforced belief in the rally.

It is however very much part of the culture of financial markets to *encourage* this rigidity of thought. The somewhat vulgar phrase, meant as complimentary, that someone "held on to their balls" encapsulates an admiration for maintaining belief in an original proposition in the face of prevailing evidence to the contrary. Smith believes a stock to be under-priced (a proposition held as knowledge), buys the stock and then sees its price collapse. Now either Smith can update his belief, concede that he was mistaken and liquidate the position or he can 'hold on to his balls', ignore the unfortunate recent events and wait for his original belief to be borne out by a dramatic rise the price. The culture of the financial markets is certainly to laud the latter approach; after all it is tougher to take a lot of financial pain on the way down and then to 'ride it' all the way up again, than to cut the losses at the first sign of trouble. But the effect of this cultural preference is undoubtedly to encourage an obstinacy that colours judgement. It eliminates the possibility of a Bayesian style updating of probabilistic belief in the light of fresh evidence, in favour of absolutist intractability.[38] When the market participants collectively act in this manner, the results can be wildly destructive.

6.

There is a theoretical construct in economic thought known as perfect competition. This is a hypothetical market situation in which barriers to entry for producers and consumers do not exist. Information is perfectly and freely available to all, in real time. Transaction costs are zero. From this set-up, thought experiments can be conducted to show how profits to producers reach an equilibrium point (known as 'normal' rather than 'super' profits) such that no-one else is encouraged to enter the market (as their addition to supply would reduce prices and eliminate the meagre remaining profits). And it has often been claimed that the markets that were thought in actuality to most closely resemble this model of perfection were the financial markets. In particular, the extraordinary timeliness of prices for products and the instant dissemination of data echoed the perfectively competitive environment.

But as one studies the theories of finance rather than those of economics, one finds that it is the very *imperfect* nature of the markets and information about them which are given prominence. Asymmetric holdings of information intuitively offer a better starting point from which to investigate why trading occurs, why prices rise or fall, how asset bubbles occur etc., etc. After all, if information is perfectly assimilated by all concerned, it is not clear why trading would so readily occur. A reasonable presumption upon which to build any explanatory theory in this field ought to recognise that both buyer and seller believe they are fairing better than the other from the exchange. Asymmetric information may therefore be a sensible assumption.

And yet, perhaps an even richer understanding is available by considering knowledge as opposed to mere information. Recognising that knowledge is a critical part of the financial markets and that there are peculiarities that serve to complicate matters relating to the acquisition of knowledge, paints the situation in a rather different light to the picture inherited loosely from the economists' image of a near-perfect, free and paradigmatic trading utopia. Indeed there are very many idiosyncratic limitations on financial market participants with regards to their capacity to procure knowledge; the narrow confines in which sensory perception may operate effectively, the insignificance of memory set against the great expanse of time and history of the markets, the inconclusiveness of inductive reasoning and the perils of applying sound theories to unstable reality. And all this before any consideration is given to the infallibility of the senses, of memory and of reasoning in the heat of a dealing room. Not all these features pertain solely to knowledge sought in the financial markets, but enough do to suggest far more philosophical work must be done in this field. It is quite astonishing that the study of an industry where knowledge is of paramount importance has not begun to consider the findings of epistemologists, the product of over two millennia of pontification.

Chapter 8

1.

There are fundamentally only two ways to proceed when confronted with a problem that is not well understood. The first is to accept the current theories or hypotheses relating to the matter and attempt to reconcile them with the troublesome observations. This entails persisting with the current paradigm, accepting the conceptual basis upon which it was formulated and adapting it only minimally and at the margins to try to make it sit comfortably with the currently inexplicable data. There are extremely good reasons for pursuing this course of action rather than the alternative (see below). It provides an incrementally progressive methodology, which builds upon previous work and energy expended. There are advantages that come from focussing or specialising on one potential solution to a problem (the division of labour principle once again) and a momentum can be created that pushes theories onward, improving them. It is by this process that societal leaders, thinkers, scientists and business leaders propel their respective fields forwards in the majority of circumstances. If we consider the problems we face in our daily working or even personal lives, it is usually by a relatively risk-averse and only gradual amendment of our current perspective that we attempt to resolve difficulties.

However, counter-factual data or news that consistently runs against the grain of our current, working hypothesis can become so overwhelming as to make the temperate approach suboptimal or even perilous. When evidence contrary to the predictions of our theory persists, despite efforts to modify and extend its scope, the need arises to question the paradigm itself. No longer will it suffice to accept unremittingly the assumptions and concepts embedded in the existing framework, through which of course our perception of the issues at hand is filtered. Eventually, it can be necessary to eject the old ideas wholesale, in favour of a radically altered mindset.

This distinction was expounded in Thomas Kuhn's dramatically influential 1963 work in the philosophy of science, *The Structure of Scientific Revolutions*. But whilst his ideas were aimed at the history of science, their applicability to all areas of intellectual endeavour was quickly recognised. It is not difficult to find scientific examples that neatly illustrate Kuhn's model; the collapse of Ptolemaic geocentric astronomy in favour of the Copernican heliocentric or the eventual collapse of Newtonian mechanical and gravitational theories following Einstein's relativistic revelations. These were shifts in the existing paradigms so significant as to render comparisons between them futile. In a sense, the disparate theories were construed in different conceptual languages such as to be incommensurable.

Kuhn's ideas were controversial; not least in so far as he considered the necessary rejection of failing paradigms to be hampered by human psychology which was averse to risk and unwilling to concede defeat. It is obvious why this would upset practising scientists, given that Kuhn thought paradigms could last decades or centuries but that they could be erroneously propagated in part due to the stubbornness and peer-pressurizing nature of adherents to the contemporary dogma. It is furthermore disquieting, if one views Kuhn's theory from a pessimistic perspective, to think that one's lifetime of research has been spent barking up the wrong tree and indeed stalling human attainment of true knowledge.

This is for philosophers and practitioners alike to debate. But regardless of the consequences of these ideas, their explanatory power is considerable. Beyond science, we typically see political solutions to problems gently amended and refined, but then observe a revolution such as occurred in Russia in 1917. In such cases, every element of the previously accepted norms can be revised or obliterated. Comparisons before and after the event, do struggle to retain their full meaningfulness. A metaphor, (or even literal instance of the theory) might be a married couple who muddle along and resolve conflicts within the context of the marriage until one or both decide that this conceptual backdrop has not only become inadequate but possibly also part of the problem. Divorce would be a paradigm shift in this case.

The recurrent problems experienced with respect to the financial markets should provoke similar anxieties. Our understanding of their workings and the subsequent regulatory frameworks we draft, are time and again proving inadequate. With each new observation or data-point, typically a credit crisis, a series of institutional failures, currency implosion etc., we attempt to update the existing paradigm. All definitions are left as before, concepts go unchallenged; extra regulation is created, but then often repealed at a later date as asset bubbles arise, profits in the sector balloon correspondingly and the influence of bankers and the like strengthens. There is an intensely strong fatalistic spirit that pervades the financial markets; an almost mythic resignation that markets cycle and history repeats. But the idea of being 'doomed' to repeat the history is part of a *conditional* warning. We are not doomed to repeat history as those in the markets seem determined to believe *unless* we ignore the lessons of history. Part of this learning should be constituted by an acceptance that the paradigm needs to shift. This book argues for a complete overhaul of our thinking towards financial markets rather than a mere tinkering at the periphery. We must abandon any concept that has not been rigorously tested and this must include every aspect of our current outlook.

2.

The events and consequences of the upheaval in financial markets in 2008 should have made their underlying importance to our daily lives patently clear. The effects of a full collapse of the modern financial system would be truly abominable. Akin to natural disasters that wreck public utilities, civil law and order would probably start to fail rapidly. Martial law would need to be established, and without swift stabilisation wars between nations would become likely in due course. This we can all assume by reference to nations or regions subject in the past to full or partial monetary collapse. It would be mistaken to think that modernity in itself is a barrier that would prevent descent into such chaos. The bungled humanitarian effort in New Orleans and subsequent societal collapse following Hurricane Katrina in 2005 should dispel any such complacency the West may feel in this regard.

To the extent that the result of financial market failure is unthinkable, the case for considering them as public utilities is all the stronger. Whilst we do not see an unbridgeable gap between the interests of private ownership and public goods, we are generally well served by a good system of regulation for privatised utilities. This is not simply to posit an *analogy* between financial systems and say national electricity grids or telecommunications networks, but to suggest that on reflection we may believe money and the financial network of banks, instruments and technologies are intrinsically of imperative public concern. This contrasts heavily with our historic stance which is to simply consider banks and the like as private businesses dealing in the commodity of money.

The issue of moral hazard was raised repeatedly during the recent crisis. Its origin is less in moral philosophy and more in behavioural economics, and refers to the tendency to act in one manner when conscious that one only bears partial responsibility for the consequences as opposed to another manner when one is fully responsible. Its relevance in relation to the bank rescue of 2008 was that the unambiguous commitment of society to bail out failing banks and other collapsing financial firms created an indelible impression as to the extent to which these institutions were tacitly underwritten. In other words, it was made explicit that banks would not be fully accountable for their actions. The result is moral hazard; the future action of banks would be predicated on the fact that their actual responsibility is, in practical reality, only partial.

For some this was reason enough to oppose the bailouts. But this position was illogical if one accepted that systemic collapse was likely without assistance, for the only reason to deny state aid on the grounds of moral hazard is out of concern for a systemic collapse in the future that its provision would engender. This is equivalent to opting for a definite collapse now, for fear of a possible collapse later. The approach taken was perfectly logical to this extent and the existence of moral hazard should now be affirmed. Optimistically, this is a position of strength in so far as it can be used to predict behaviour; uncertainty as to whether or not banks will be allowed to fail *en masse* in a crisis seems largely to have been removed. In short, they won't. But pragmatically, this new state of affairs must be accounted for in any philosophical or abstract investigation into the financial markets and their behaviour.

A thorough revision of our methodology for studying the markets is imperative. Ignorance is never preferable to knowledge in matters that are not inevitable. Our current age is one of discovery in every imaginable field on an unprecedented scale. New methods of research are evolving, opportunities for synergies across disciplines are increasing, and information can be processed and exchanged more rapidly than ever before. These are tremendously exciting times in the intellectual story of mankind. But for our understanding of finance to keep pace, it requires a far more profound renewal of its methodology; its breadth and depth must be substantially increased and its philosophical basis established.

The risks from not acting to reduce the lag that finance theory exhibits will come not simply from the markets as we know them or the seemingly inevitable effects of moral hazard. There is an extent to which society ought to attempt to future-proof itself from the potentially harmful and as yet unknowable consequences of still to be constructed financial devices. Historically, extrapolating from the contemporary set of entities, instruments, technologies, people and concepts in the financial markets has given very little long term insight into what is around the corner. Credit default swaps, which featured prevalently in the recent crisis, were practically unheard of before 1997. Collateralized debt obligations only originated in 1987. It would be unwise to think that the next generations of traders and brokers will not devise new games with new rules. Even generalisations regarding the type of persons who will be involved in the market will be contestable. In the City of London the stereotypical image of old Etonian stockbrokers gave way in the late 1980s to that of the East End barrow boy before the recruitment drive in the 1990s demanded economists, mathematicians and finance theorists before yet another change towards computer scientists and quants in the early 2000s. As technology evolves, its application in the markets becomes ever more widespread; the study of the effects of such changes is in its infancy. New products are constantly being created, ostensibly to satisfy a supposed demand or reduce risk in some way, yet history teaches us that these instruments can seem to take on a scope of existence far and beyond that originally intended. At times it can appear that new instruments or concepts seem to lead to a conjuring up of dramatic profits for the institutions involved. The source of these apparent winnings needs meticulous scrutinizing; their genuine capacity to reduce economic or commercial risks needs better determination; of their being merely another face of leveraged speculation, we must be ever vigilant.

I have argued that finance theory and practice has no serious philosophical basis and that there are many historical reasons why this is the case. I have suggested some of the many questions that are raised when one starts to contemplate the financial markets from a formal, philosophical standpoint. It should be clear that such questions are not merely interesting as abstract diversions but are utterly critical to our attempts to understand the markets. The paradigm shift that must occur in our thinking is far removed from the shallow inquiry that has generally been made since the recent crisis or the lamentable finessing of existing regulatory frameworks. The metaphysical nature of the entities, instruments and concepts that seem to exist in the financial markets are profoundly different from those of other industries. We must probe far more deeply into the implications resulting from these differences. We must not shy away from debates as to the ethics of financial market activity nor approach them with unhelpful preconceptions, or worse, with a solely retributive mindset. We must attempt to turn to society's genuine advantage the industry's extraordinary ability to innovate and to convince very smart people to work exceedingly hard and under oppressive circumstances, rather than to act simply as lender of last resort. And from those who claim that society already benefits to a marvellous degree from the industry as is, we ought to ask that the evidence be presented more cogently and less obliquely than has hitherto been the case. The industry's traditional pointing to tax receipts in this regard can be comprehensively dismissed following the massive liabilities assumed by taxpayers in its preservation.

3.

If our approach to matters surrounding the financial markets is accepted as inadequate and is deemed to compare unfavourably with our means of addressing other affairs, and if furthermore it is admitted that these shortcomings substantially elevate the risk of recurring crises and impair our aversive capacities, then it is imperative that we act to amend the situation. As has been variously claimed, repeating an action over and over and expecting different results is a form of madness. But how explicitly should we proceed? The assertions made in this book do not suggest that a quick fix is available such as to mitigate the problems we face immediately. This is to be expected, given the source of the insufficiencies are deeply and historically ingrained. Nevertheless, we must start somewhere and the sooner we do so the better. Here then is something of an action plan; a rare thing one suspects in philosophical circles.

Firstly the nature of the problem needs due recognition. Until it is accepted that the manner in which we analyse and legislate the financial markets is anomalous and that a deep consideration of their being must be conducted, progress cannot be expected. Whilst issues of political expedience or plain ignorance may explain the continued use of woefully simplified analysis, dispensing with the language of parody and untested presumption, is a first step to shifting the paradigm. We must concede that the clinical reality of the trillions of dollars, pounds and euros placed at risk is keenly at odds with the childish recriminatory tone employed universally; it is bewildering how 'greedy' or 'reckless' can be thought adequate or appropriate set against a bailout of such magnitude.

On accepting the error of our ways, we must then begin on a new methodological path. Nothing must be held to be beyond renewed inquiry. The questions posed in this book regarding ontology, epistemology and ethics are merely indicative of the wholesale revision that is required. We must ask what markets truly are, what they are for, what they *ought* to be for. We have to begin to analyse financial markets in the wider societal context and ask how they strictly relate to other businesses and to political matters. We should consider the case for their inclusion as a public utility. In approaching these philosophical matters, we must draw on the best knowledge acquired by research in modern science, social science and the humanities. This is very much an approach that the field of philosophy has always encouraged; when questions arise it is often in a philosophical context, but if the practical sciences can provide answers or refine the questions themselves, then this should be welcomed.

These are the general and primary changes that must be made before other, substantive alterations to our current perspective can occur. We must formally establish the Philosophy of Finance as a stand-alone academic subject. There is no single prescription in this book of greater importance than this. The study of philosophical issues relating to finance must be a cross-disciplinary effort, as experts in both fields, at least initially, will be few in number. In other faculties, the philosophers of individual subjects are often specialists in the field with a philosophical bent; a biologist perhaps who becomes interested in the more abstract and fundamental principles of the field. But there is nothing to stop philosophers *qua* philosophers interesting themselves in finance; indeed that is to be encouraged. And to re-affirm, the philosophy of finance is not an especially peculiar idea; it is its current non-existence which is remarkable and lamentable. Initially, the philosophy of finance will start with questions, a sample of which has been offered in this book. Establishing new subjects in this manner is really no difficult matter; the Economics of the Internet for example became a recognised sub-branch of economic theory shortly after web-based commerce became a reality. Alongside the philosophy of finance, the history of financial markets and the history of finance theory must be given far greater emphasis than is currently the case. The history of the subject (practical and academic) should form a compulsory module for any post- or undergraduate degree rather than a rare optional course. Regarding ethics, until the moral philosophical aspect of the financial markets has a sizeable literature of its own, students would be well-served attending applied or theoretical ethics classes taught in philosophy departments. Finance modules teaching quantitative techniques and mathematical modelling for trading should include lecturing on the philosophy of science to increase awareness of the fallibility of statistical methods and to highlight the abstract differences between scientific analysis and numerical finance. Reading lists generally must cease to be contrived only to include technical work descendant from Chicago economics. Until Ruskin, Steinbeck, Pope, Drucker and Hazlitt are read as commonly as Friedman, Markowitz, Fama and Sharpe by prospective financiers, the likelihood of the industry itself broadening its horizons and considering its impact on society is minimal.

We must unashamedly begin a dialogue on ethical matters with respect to the financial markets. We must abandon preconceptions and commence such talks without preconditions. Society cannot continue to express moral indignation without full provision of the charges brought against financiers. Nor should bankers and traders be allowed exemption from morally justifying their own actions by vaguely asserting a by-product that enriches society. We must ask to what end the various types of trading occur and what risks or benefits they bring. Whilst maintaining a spirit of tolerance, we should nevertheless not refrain from professing certain activities to be worthier than others, if we feel it to be so; we are comfortable enough to do this in other areas of life. We must be pragmatic and acknowledge that the financial markets attract persons with certain traits and by the nature of the activities themselves, make particular demands of workers; to this end we must assess the likelihood of the industry self-regulating with suitable efficacy for society as a whole. And we must not be afraid to fail, particular as regards regulation. The effects of Laws of Unintended Consequences are unavoidable. But the alternative, *laissez-faire* approach brought us to the point of near collapse. We shall need to be prepared to be more radical than ever before as the effects of a thorough catastrophe are unthinkable. Increasing mandatory bank capital reserves from single-digit percentages to low double-digit percentages hardly fits the required revolutionary bill. Discussion of exceedingly narrow banking or fully mutualised banking or of 100% capital reserve banking is more in keeping with the radicalism we must contemplate. This requires the courage and liberality of original, intelligent thought. It requires an invocation of the intellectual spirit that is the hallmark of seemly, heroic, philosophical contemplation.

NOTES

[1] "All men are heterosexual" is a strong claim. It requires a weak counter-claim by which to be refuted e.g. "Gary is a homosexual". In contrast, "Some men are heterosexual" is a weaker claim and, therefore, requires a strong counter-claim to be refuted.

[2] Although having had their fingers burnt on several such 'investments' earlier in the crisis, such funding was not readily forthcoming; in hindsight this was a missed opportunity for the East.

[3] "There is but one truly serious philosophical problem and that is suicide. Judging whether life is or is not worth living amounts to answering the fundamental question of philosophy. All the rest – whether or not the world has three dimensions, whether the mind has nine or twelve categories – comes afterwards". Albert Camus, *The Myth of Sisyphus*, translation published by Hamish Hamilton, 1955.

[4] To such promulgation, 'Modern Art' is likely to be considered formally question-begging, since the artfulness of Modern Art is precisely what is at issue.

[5] Although as Marcus Aurelius observed, the need to make good decisions in all haste, as urgent circumstances dictate, is precisely why lifelong philosophical training is necessary.

[6] These claims are of the precise sort that, it will later be claimed, should be thoroughly revised and re-considered. For now, their truth or otherwise is inessential, since it is the *perception* that they are true that has brought this subject matter to the attention of economists first and foremost.

[7] Sound familiar? That history has repeated itself so swiftly is partially explicable by the extraordinary ignorance of new entrants to the market. *Cf* George Santayana's famous quotation regarding those condemned to repeat history.

[8] Occam's Razor is the idea that parsimony of explanation is desirable. If something can be explained without certain assumptions being made, then the assumptions should be eliminated from the hypothesis. The idea has been highly influential in modern scientific and intellectual endeavour.

[9] Formally it is to commit the fallacy of affirming the consequent. This is to assert "If A then B", "B", therefore "A". In this case: "If philosophers and bankers are uninterested in the philosophy of finance, there will be no papers in journals on the subject. There are no papers on the subject, therefore they are uninterested."

[10] Indeed, one might (controversially) trace the social sciences back to biology, thence on to chemistry and further still to physics. At the edge of physics, beyond the cosmological and quantum, lies metaphysics; when the questions as to what exist blend with those asking why fore.

[11] See succeeding discussion on value and price.

[12] The complexity or obscurity of a counterfactual example does not affect its capacity to contradict a hypothesis.

[13] For a full explanation, see a good introductory textbook on option theory. Here, for the curious, is a brief summary. If, collectively, option market makers are especially long options of a particular strike and they hedge their associated theta decay by gamma trading, whilst the end users (or paper as they are called), collectively, are short the same strike and NOT hedging their *short* gamma position, the net effect is to pin the futures to the strike. The reason for this is that a rise in prices away from the strike encourages the option market makers to hedge their long deltas occurring as a result of gamma i.e. to sell futures, and a fall in futures prices encourages them to buy futures via the same mechanism in reverse, whilst the paper, by not hedging, do not cancel out the market maker trades. This can also become self-fulfilling if the futures are thought to be pinning, the market makers will tend to hedge tighter and tighter to the strike thus sealing their own fate; and as the futures wander less and less far from the strike, short gamma players are less inclined to hedge in the opposite direction. Finally, it is not uncommon for non-option players in the futures market to be aware of expiry day effects such as these and adjust behaviour accordingly. "Triple-witching" in the US is a particular case of this.

[14] There are limits to this particular analogy. Would horse racing exist as a sport without gamblers? Although it undoubtedly could, feedback between the 'derivative' and 'underlying' seems to be a property that emerges when the derivative market becomes lively.

[15] This distinction is as old as philosophy itself; the earliest pre-Socratic philosophers focussed on natural philosophy, a proto-scientific method. Moral and normative philosophy emerges predominantly from Socrates onwards.

[16] Aristotle, *Politics*, I.11, OUP, 1995, p32

[17] One may wonder why so many recommendations are necessary when the client generally simply wants to know whether he should buy or sell. One might suggest that the effect of all these gradations is to reduce the strength of any one particular recommendation that a broker might make. An ACCUMULATE recommendation that precedes falling prices might for some seem to be less directly or semantically contradicted than an outright BUY recommendation.

[18] Transitivity is a logical rule such that if A=B and B=C then A=C.

[19] The time value of money refers to the notion that money has different values relative to time. Specifically, a pound today is worth more than a pound a year from now, other things being equal, since it can be placed on risk-free interest bearing deposit. Thus the value of future money from the standpoint of today needs to be discounted by an appropriate factor, usually approximated by the interest rate curve. A bird in the hand (today) is worth two in the bush (tomorrow), one might say.

[20] Laplace posited the existence of an omniscient demon that knew the location and velocity of every particle in the Universe and could therefore, theoretically, forecast every occurrence forevermore. Laplace's demon has acute relevance in the problem of free will under determinism. For if the demon is a theoretical possibility, it might be argued that free will is a theoretical impossibility, since any action one thinks one chooses would have been foreseen and predicted by the demon.

[21] Kaufman, H, *The Road to Financial Reformation,*

[22] Strawson, P, *Freedom and Resentment*

[23] Smith, A, *The Wealth of Nations*

[24] Plato's theory of forms or Universals is the cornerstone of his metaphysics, which saw the *essence* of the world and its contents as an idealised Form or Universal, of which actual objects were pale imitations. A virtuous life in Plato's mind was one devoted to the contemplation of these Universals.

[25] A trader was accosted by a woman at a party who had seen him pull up in his Ferrari. "Of course you know what they say about traders with big cars?" she asked, provocatively. "Yes", the trader replied. "They have fucking big houses".

[26] Note the syntax here follows the financial market convention. Buyers pay price for quantity. Sellers sell quantity at price. This can be traced to open-outcry trading linguistics and the evolution of a system that minimised confusion over whether one was buying or selling. "6 for 100!" means "I'm willing to pay 6 for 100 lots" whereas "100 at 6" means "I can sell 100 lots at 6". This is very rapid and clear; for=buyer, at=seller.

[27] For derivatives geeks, the only one that springs to my mind is to look for a 10 year straddle on the spread that is trading at or near to zero. Do let me know if you find one.

[28] Sorkin, A, *Too Big To Fail*, p447

[29] Franciscan and Dominican mendicant monks respectively.

[30] Wisdom, temperance, courage and justice.

[31] 'Virtuous man' is somewhat tautological, etymologically speaking. Virtue derives from *vir* meaning man.

[32] It is hard to see how any devout Christian can trade in the financial markets for a living.

[33] The productive efficacy of capitalism is largely a corollary to the division of labour principle, which, as mentioned earlier, is practically axiomatic i.e. self-evidently true.

[34] Evidently formally question begging.

[35] Hume, David, *A Treatise of Human Nature,* Book III, Part I, Sec I

[36] Since the 1980s, the massive increase in the use of automated or black box systems renders this assumption increasingly doubtful in this particular form.

[37] Except perhaps accountancy and actuarial work, where the reasons are altogether far more compelling given the nature of that which is being studied.

[38] 18th century British mathematician Thomas Bayes derived a theorem connecting a conditional probability with its inverse. A conditional probability is the likelihood of an event given some other fact. Its inverse is the likelihood of observing the fact given the initial event. Bayesian statistics employs this relation by considering the likelihood of an event in the light of new information. Given the new information has been observed, it updates the probability of the initial event.